Your Expert Guide
to common problems & how to fix them

MG Midget & A-H Sprite

Sprite MkI, II, III, IV & Austin
Sprite, 1958 to 1971
Midget MkI, II, III & Midget
1500, 1961 to 1979

Your marque expert
Terry Horler

MG/A-H
Midget/Sprite

Other great books from Veloce –

www.veloce.co.uk/www.velocebooks.com

First published in June 2012, reprinted August 2020 by Veloce, an imprint of David and Charles Limited. Tel +44 (0)1305 260068 / e-mail info@veloce.co.uk / web www.veloce.co.uk.

ISBN: 978-1-845844-02-8

Throughout this book logos, model names and designations, etc, have been used for the purposes of identification, illustration and decoration. Such names are the property of the trademark holder as this is not an official publication. Readers with ideas for automotive books, or books on other transport or related hobby subjects, are invited to write to the editorial director of Veloce at the above email address. British Library Cataloguing in Publication Data – A catalogue record for this book is available from the British Library. Design and DTP by Veloce. Printed and bound by CPI Group (UK) Ltd, Croydon, CR0 4YY.

This book is not intended to replace your workshop manual, or to tell you how to service and/or repair your Midget or Sprite. It is intended to give you an understanding of the things that can go wrong in service, and how to diagnose faults that you or a third party can then set about repairing. In the most part, Midgets and Sprites are very simple cars, and quite easy to work on. They are also very reliable when properly serviced. However, anything can go wrong with an elderly vehicle, and unlike modern vehicles where a mechanic (sorry, technician), will start by plugging in the diagnostic computer, you'll find no such socket on a Spridget.

Whatever your normal diagnostic approach (be it old-fashioned belt and braces diagnostics, gut instinct, or educated guesswork – or do you just simply wait until something drops off?) this book will help with a more methodical approach. Although it assumes that you already have some basic knowledge of how your car works, and the terminology associated with 20th century cars, I have tried to keep things simple, and guide you to the area of your car and/or the section in your workshop manual that will identify the issue.

Introduced in 1958, the Sprite drew many of its constituent components from the Austin A35 saloon. This used the British Motor Corporation (BMC) A-series engine and gearbox, and, with the simple addition of a small pair of SU carburettors, produced 42.5bhp, which was deemed sufficient to have some fun with; well, for a while anyway. Over the next few years power and engine capacity grew, and the engine was modified further from the main BMC saloon cars and commercials that shared the basic design. In October 1974, the A-series engine and gearbox

unit was replaced by the 1493cc Triumph Spitfire engine and gearbox – the Spridget's arch rival joining the BMC family when Leyland, the Spitfire's parent, amalgamated with BMC to become British Leyland in 1968. The change of engine was dictated by the need to meet the new North American emissions regulations; the Midget's largest single market.

Spridgets have always been much modified by their owners; indeed, very few remained in factory specification for more than a few hours from new it seemed! Some modifications are well thought through and highly desirable, others may be poorly thought out, poorly applied, and even downright dangerous. All can affect performance, economy, reliability and safety. We'll look at some of the more popular modifications as we work through the book, but for a general overview of modifications, please refer to Chapter 16. Modified examples can be a law unto themselves, and each must be approached on its own merits. You may need to seek expert advice for your own particular example if extensively modified.

Thanks

I would like to thank the following for their help and patience: David Polonowski (www.david.polonowski.com), who took the majority of the photographs for this book; the many Sprite and Midget owners who allowed us to poke into every nook and cranny of their cars; The Midget and Sprite Club (www.midgetandspriteclub.com); and Peter May Engineering (www.petermayengineering.co.uk).

Contents

All versions used a four-cylinder, in-line, overhead valve engine, with two valves per cylinder and three main bearings supporting the crankshaft. The cylinder block and cylinder head were produced in cast iron, and a pressed steel sump pan contained the oil for a fully pressurised lubrication system though a full-flow

Dating from 1951 and designed for the Austin A30 saloon with an initial capacity of 803cc, the A-series engine proved to be a reliable and economical unit for the Spridgets in 948, 1098 and 1275cc capacities. The external features of the A-series engine changed little during that time.

The 1493cc Triumph Spitfire engine replaced the A-series engine from October 1974. The Triumph engine can trace its origins back to 1953 for the then new Standard 8 saloon with a capacity of 803cc. Various enlargements over the years saw this engine used in both Standard and Triumph vehicles. As applied to the 1974 Midget, it offered an easier solution to comply with ever more stringent North American emissions regulations while still providing reasonable performance.

oil filter. A single chain-driven camshaft operated the vertically-placed valves via eight pushrods. Induction and exhaust ports were placed to one side of the cylinder head. From 1958 to October 1974, the engine was a BMC A-series unit of 948cc, 1098cc and finally 1275cc capacity. The induction and exhaust systems were placed on the left-hand side of the engine, with distributor and dynamo/alternator on the right-hand side. From October 1974, the Triumph 1493cc was used, the above ancillary items being transposed to the opposite sides.

1. Engine starting problems

For the engine to start, the following conditions must exist:
• Adequate electrical power to maintain a sufficient cranking speed to turn the engine, while at the same time providing sufficient power to the ignition system and, if applicable, the electric fuel pump. If the cranking speed is low or strained, please refer to the electrical chapter.
• A good spark at each sparkplug and at the correct point on the compression stroke. (Please refer to the ignition system chapter).
• The correct delivery of the fuel-to-air ratio from the carburettors. (Please refer to the fuel system chapter).
• A healthy compression ratio within the combustion chamber at cranking speed. We'll look at this item here.

2. Low compression

An engine will never perform properly if the compression ratio is reduced on one or more cylinders. Performance will be reduced, fuel consumption will increase, and the engine will run less smoothly, possibly very unevenly. The engine may not achieve a consistent cranking speed on the starter motor if one or more cylinders are losing compression.

The only way to be certain is to use a compression gauge on

The engine should be hot when carrying out a compression test. Remove all sparkplugs and test with the throttle fully open. Have an assistant operate the starter until a maximum pressure reading is obtained. For safety, disable the ignition (pull an LT lead from the coil) to prevent any arcing at the HT leads.

each cylinder and to compare the readings. Check the maximum pressure reading on each cylinder, any more than a 10 per cent discrepancy between cylinders is a sure sign that the engine is ailing. A compression test should be carried out when the engine is at normal operating temperature and with the throttle fully open. Ensure that the ignition is inoperative, a HT lead could produce a spark to earth with the plugs removed, and any fuel vapour expelled through an open plug hole could ignite. The pressure should be in the order of 8.0 bar or above, dependant upon the individual version or if modified, any reading below this will need further investigation. Certainly, a reading considerably less than this will manifest itself in poor running and starting performance.

An uneven exhaust beat will be heard if one or more cylinders are suffering a significant loss of compression. A low compression pressure may be caused by badly seating valves, a leaking cylinder head gasket or worn cylinder bores, piston rings and pistons. The cylinder head must be removed to ascertain which, or any combination of these, is the culprit. If the engine has a high oil consumption with blue smoke visible from the exhaust, then a full engine rebuild may well be required. However, if the crankcase ventilation system is not functioning correctly, this too may cause high oil consumption. Not only will a reduced compression pressure make starting more difficult, but excess oil within the combustion space will foul the sparkplug. If a sparkplug looks black and oil wetted, then this is a fair indication that oil is getting past the piston rings or valve guides. If the engine fails to start within half a dozen attempts or so, investigate before exhausting the battery or fouling the sparkplugs with fuel or oil.

The 1493cc is the only Spridget engine to have valve seat inserts fitted at manufacture. This gives it a better resistance to valve seat recession caused by unleaded fuel. Even so, better grade valve seat inserts were fitted for the North American versions. Unless upgraded valve seat inserts have been fitted to a home market version, use a fuel additive.

3. Cylinder head gasket

Head gasket failure is not a particular problem with any of these engines unless fairly drastically modified. The 1275cc engine can be bored out to 1380cc making the land between the middle two cylinders very narrow indeed. If the compression ratio has been significantly increased then this too increases the chances of a failure between cylinders. If the engine has severely overheated

'Mayonnaise' build-up within the rocker cover is not unusual in cold conditions. If excessive, as here and also on the dipstick, suspect that the cylinder head gasket is leaking.

due to a cooling system fault, then this is the most likely cause for the head gasket to fail.

When a head gasket fails, it may not necessarily affect the cooling system, so the usual checks of cross contamination of oil and water or expulsion of water from the radiator pressure cap may not reveal anything. Check if the colour of combustion deposit on each sparkplug is the same. (Refer to Chapter 5 page 37 to see other causes for differences in combustion deposit colour). Hence a compression test is vital. White smoke from the exhaust when the engine is fully warmed up is another clue to a leaking cylinder head gasket. All engines can produce white

Valve and valve seats must be in good order for an engine to run properly. Consider fitting hardened valve seat inserts so that you can use unleaded fuel instead of a fuel additive.

smoke when cold, or during damp and cold weather conditions, but this should clear once fully warmed.

Check for a creamy semifluid 'mayonnaise' build-up within the rocker cover and oil filler cap. Again, this is not unusual in cold and damp conditions, or for an engine that seldom reaches full operating temperature for long. If excessive, then this may indicate that moisture is contaminating the engine oil.

Check the dipstick as well for 'mayonnaise' build-up. This could be caused by a leak in the cylinder head gasket, or a blockage in the engine breather pipework. With the cylinder head removed, check for even colouring of each piston – if coolant has been getting into a cylinder, the affected piston head will look cleaner than is usual.

4. Valve seating problems

Poorly seating valves may be caused by the use of unleaded fuel without a suitable additive, or the lack of suitably hardened valve

seats. The hammering effect of the valves against the seat, compounded by the high combustion gas temperature, makes a very hostile environment, especially for the exhaust valves. Incorrect valve clearances, or an engine running with the incorrect ignition or fuel/air ratio can lead to valve burning and valve seat damage. Again, a modified engine with a high lift/overlap camshaft, stronger valve springs and producing a higher combustion temperature can all contribute toward increased valve seating problems.

5. Lubrication problems

Modern synthetic engine oils are not suitable for these engines. Due to the design and running clearances, 20W/50 multigrade oils are the safest choice. The oil pressure gauge, when fitted, should indicate pressure almost immediately on start-up, and maintain the pressure stated in the handbook/workshop manual. If the pressure reading is low, sluggish to build, and accompanied by knocking or rumbling noises, then a rebuild will not be far away. The 1493cc is particularly prone to crankshaft bearing wear, and intolerant to prolonged usage in this condition (it can throw a connecting rod through the cylinder block). The earlier 948cc crankshaft can suffer breakage.

All of these engines will consume oil, and topping up between regular oil changes is normal. An oil consumption of 800 miles

Peter May Engineering produce this rear crankshaft oil seal modification to help cure the notorious oil leakage problem on the A-series engine.

per pint is not excessive for these units, but anything less than 500 miles indicates a tired engine. A trace of blue smoke from the exhaust will certainly be evident at this level.

It is quite common for the A-series engine to develop leaks, particularly at the rear crankshaft seal and front pulley seal. These can be difficult to cure, although a modified rear seal kit is available, incorporating a lip seal in replacement housing. The 948 and 1098cc engines can suffer oil leakage from the two pressed steel tappet chest covers behind the exhaust manifold. The covers distort with age, and from persistent over-tightening in attempting to cure leakage. The 10cc and early 12cc type engines used a 'Smiths' recirculatory crankcase ventilation valve fitted to the inlet manifolds. The valve contains a rubber diaphragm which, over time, can perish and develop cracks. Oil can then be drawn into the inlet manifold, the resultant blue smoke from the exhaust giving the impression of a very badly worn engine. If fitted, always check the condition of the diaphragm before fearing the worst. Many owners have subsequently dispensed with this valve and either reverted to venting to atmosphere, or changed to the later type SU carburettors with venting connections

Whichever type of venting arrangement is used, ensure that all pipework, breathers and oil-filler cap breathers are in good order and compatible to the system used. Mixing or modifying the type

The Smiths recirculatory valve allows crankcase gases into the inlet manifold. This replaced venting to atmosphere as a first step toward emissions control. Ensure the rubber pipes and connections to and from the valve are in good order and not leaking. A leak can upset the carburetion as well as the escape of oil fumes.

of breathing system can cause venting and running problems. A poorly venting engine may suffer contamination of the lubricating oil and over-pressurisation of the crankcase, leading to excessive oil leakage.

6. Oil pressure relief valve

The A-series engine has an accessible oil pressure relief valve. This is situated at the rear of the cylinder block on the right-hand side, just below the external oil pipe to the oil filter head. A weak relief spring or poorly seating valve may prevent the oil pressure from attaining the correct figure. The spring and valve can be removed for inspection by unscrewing the large hexagonal plug. A low oil pressure on an otherwise healthy engine may be due to the relief valve bleeding off too much oil to return to the sump. A popular modification is to replace the cone-shaped valve with a ball bearing – this sometimes provides a better seating in the block. Spring length is critical to maintain the correct pressure; replacing the valve with a ball will require a different spring length. Too high an oil pressure reading will almost certainly be caused by too long a spring length. Some owners may pack out the valve and spring with washers, thus increasing the pressure on an engine with incorrect pressure caused by worn bearings. If the pressure appears to be correct, but the engine is knocking, rumbling and generally sounding tired, the relief valve may have been tampered with in an attempt to disguise this.

7. Oil filtration

Prior to 1970, a replaceable element oil filter was employed; the filter bowl can be difficult to reseal following element replacement. It is imperative to watch the oil filter on start-up – a leak here can be dramatic and catastrophic. Many owners will fit the later spin-on-type oil filter adaptor; this is not only much easier to change, but far less likely to leak. A word of warning concerning the replaceable element filter – ensure that the large washer beneath the filter element is both present and fitted the right way up. It is very easy to miss this washer; it becomes stuck to the bottom of the element and, if you are

Most importantly, ensure the larger domed washer is fitted below the replacement element oil filter, along with the spring and washers. The dome must face upward. Check for oil leaks when starting; the filter bowl can be difficult to seal properly. The spin-on-type filter used from 1970 (above right) is simple and easy to change, with far less chance of leakage, too. This is a popular modification for earlier engines, but the filter head casting must be changed to enable the use of a sealed cannister filter.

unaware of its presence, gets thrown away with the old filter. Without this washer, the element will drop to the bottom of filter bowl allowing unfiltered oil to pass over the top into the main oil gallery. The oil pressure gauge readings will not be affected until the bearings wear prematurely from the passing of unfiltered oil. Always pre-fill a new oil filter with as much fresh engine oil as you can get in without spillage. This will reduce the time for oil pressure to build on start-up. From 1964 to 1970, a small warning light was placed above the oil pressure gauge; this is the oil filter by-pass valve warning light. This will illuminate should the oil filter element become sufficiently blocked for the by-pass valve to open to maintain an oil flow. However, this will now be unfiltered oil directly from the oil pump and may contain particles that will accelerate bearing wear.

8. Oil changing intervals

When announced in 1958, the owner's handbook advised that the engine oil should be changed every 3000 miles and the filter element at 6000 mile intervals. Today, it depends more on how much you use your car. With regular usage, a change of both oil and filter at 5000 mile intervals is fine. For limited usage, a change interval of once a year should be adopted. Engine oil can absorb moisture and contaminates during storage and frequent cold starting.

Neither the BMC A-series nor Triumph 1493cc engines are as quiet and sweet as the present day engines that we have become so accustomed to. A small amount of mechanical noise is not unusual and generally nothing to worry about. However, you do need to know which noises are acceptable and those noises that spell trouble.

1. Valve train noise

Valve clearances require periodic manual adjustment as per the workshop manual. Wear in the rocker shaft, valve guides, tappet blocks and rocker faces can all contribute

The rocker shaft on all engines can wear, along with the rocker arm bearing and the rocker arm contact face where it operates the valve. A new rocker shaft and rockers will be required to cure this. Noise can also be generated by worn tappets and camshaft lobes, requiring an engine strip down job to inspect. Always fit new tappets when renewing a camshaft.

to generating audible tapping noise, even if the valve clearances appear to be set correctly. Never reduce the valve clearance to less than the stated value in an

Setting the valve clearances should only be done when the engine is cold. Never reduce the clearance in an attempt to eliminate noise. If noise persists, check for worn components. Always use a new rocker cover gasket.

attempt to eliminate any noise. This can cause premature valve sealing problems. A small amount of valve 'tap' is not unusual, but should this become excessive, then replacement parts will be required. High-performance camshafts and heavy-duty valve springs may promote a higher noise level. The rocker shaft is a common item to wear on all versions.

2. Timing chain rattle

The 948cc and 1098cc engines used a single row timing chain with a rubber tension ring set in the cam wheel. Timing chain rattle is quite common with this type and, although annoying, chain breakage is rare. The 1275cc engine used a twin row timing chain without any tensioning device and proved much longer lasting and quieter in operation. This can be retro-fitted to the smaller capacity engines with only a minor modification to the engine front plate screws. This is now a common modification. The 1493cc engine has a single row roller chain tensioned by a spring-loaded slipper blade. This is usually very reliable but eventually both chain and slipper can wear sufficiently to generate a rattle, and should be replaced.

3. Thrust washer wear

The 1493cc engine differed in having an 8 port cylinder head, compared to the 5 port head of the A-series, the latter having shared inlet ports for the front and rear pairs of cylinders and a shared exhaust port for the centre two cylinders. The oil pump was located in the sump and driven, via a pair of skew gears, from the camshaft the upper end of the shaft driving the distributor. However, the main difference and the Achilles heel of this engine is the crankshaft thrust washers, these being just half washers located either side of the rear main bearing housing. These can suffer a rapid wear rate and actually drop out of the housing when worn thin enough. The resultant wear allowed excessive end float

The A-series engine does not have a timing chain tensioner. When the chain becomes this stretched, it needs to be replaced to restore rattle-free running. Replace the crankshaft pulley oil seal at the same time.

Engine and gearbox can be removed together, or separately as shown here, engine first, followed by the gearbox. Only use substantial engine lifting equipment if attempting both together. Engine must be tipped rearwards to clear front crossmember.

of the crankshaft which, ultimately, can destroy the engine. This basic design of this engine could be traced back to 1953 as an 803cc unit of 26bhp. Stretching it to 1493cc and 65bhp was, perhaps, stretching it a little too far! Low oil pressure and bearing noise are danger signs not to be ignored. Have an assistant press the clutch pedal whilst you observe the crankshaft pulley. Any longitudinally movement, or end float, will indicate worn thrust washers.

4. Crankshaft bearing rumble and knocking
A heavy knocking or rumbling sound is indicative of crankshaft bearing wear. This may be more evident on a cold start-up, or when the engine is hot and the lubricating oil is thinner. All versions prior GAN6-200001, August 1977, were fitted with an oil pressure gauge. A low reading will certainly provide proof of a seriously worn engine.

5. Pinking or detonation rattle
A light metallic knocking sound under heavy engine load may be heard if the ignition timing is too far advanced. Referred to as 'pinging' or 'pinking', this diesel engine-like noise is caused by the charge mixture exploding (rather than burning) within the combustion chamber. This can result in valve and piston burning due to the very high temperature and shock load generated. This should be investigated immediately. Too low a fuel octane value, a weak fuel mixture, carbon build-up and an overheating engine can all contribute toward 'pinking.'

6. Piston slap

This will be a dull knocking sound, more evident when the engine is cold and before the pistons fully expanded to running temperature. This is common on engines built for competition usage where a loose fitting piston may be desirable, but can be rather more annoying on a road engine. If piston slap is heard when the engine is cold it is something you may have to live with, if the engine is healthy in every other respect. If the noise continues when hot and the oil consumption is high, then an engine rebuild may not far away.

7. Drivebelt screech

A screeching sound from the front of the engine immediately after starting is most likely a slipping fan/generator belt. The generator is under maximum load after start-up to recover the battery energy expelled during starting. An insufficiently tensioned belt can loose grip under this load. A similar noise may be experienced should the water pump bearing fail.

8. Chuffing and spluttering

More evident when the accelerator

Check the tension and condition of the fan belt if a screeching is heard when the dynamo or alternator are under heavy load, especially following initial start-up. Do not over-tighten the belt; this can shorten the life of water pump and generator bearings.

is opened and the engine is working hard, this is most likely an exhaust gas leak from around the exhaust manifold to downpipe joint. The manifold to cylinder head gasket may leak if the securing nuts are not re-tightened following a gasket replacement. If a leak is particularly bad, popping and banging may be heard on the over-run. On North American emissions control-equipped versions, check the air pump and exhaust gas recirculation pipework for any signs of leakage.

3 Clutch & gearbox

All versions use a hydraulically-operated clutch. Adjustment is automatic within the hydraulic slave cylinder. The master cylinder is located in the pedal box, and is connected via a pipe to a slave cylinder mounted on the bellhousing. A spring-type clutch is fitted to the 948cc and 1098cc engines, and a diaphragm clutch to the 1275cc and 1493cc engines. A carbon graphite thrust ring clutch release bearing is used on the 948cc, 1098cc and 1275cc engines, with a ball bearing thrust bearing on the 1493cc engine.

All gearboxes are four-speed units, only the 1493cc engine has synchromesh on first gear. The cone-type synchromesh on the 948cc engine gearbox proved rather weak. An improved gearbox with baulk ring-type synchromesh and a ribbed aluminium casing was introduced with the 1098cc engine. This proved much better in operation. The AN5 gearbox with the smooth aluminium casing was taken directly from the Austin A35, the gear ratios were less than ideal for the Sprite, with second gear being particularly low. For the HAN6/GAN1, the same casing was used but with a much improved set of ratios. This set of ratios was retained until the introduction of the 1493cc engine and an all synchromesh gearbox. The gearboxes of 948cc, 1098cc, and 1275cc engines are not interchangeable with the 1493cc gearbox. It is not uncommon to find that an early version has had the smooth casing gearbox replaced by the later and improved ribbed casing gearbox.

The A-series 'ribbed' case gearbox, used from October 1962. The cables from the gearlever extension are for the reversing light switch as fitted from September 1967.

1. Clutch not disengaging

Difficulty in selecting any gear from rest, or on the move, is a sure sign that the clutch is not disengaging fully. The clutch pedal pressure may become much lighter or develop increased travel before any pressure is felt. Firstly, check the fluid level in the master cylinder. If this has fallen then a leak has developed in the hydraulic circuit and this must be investigated. Usually, it is the slave cylinder mounted on the bellhousing that fails first. This can only be examined from underneath the car, pull back the rubber dust seal and check for hydraulic fluid leaking past the main seal in the cylinder

bore. A replacement seal can be fitted but if the bore is at all worn or corroded, then any cure could be short lived and a new slave cylinder will be required.

The slave cylinder for the Midget 1500 will have to be removed from the bellhousing to be inspected, any leakage will be internal to the housing and not visible in situ.

If the slave cylinder seal has failed, then the master cylinder seal should also be changed at the same time. Again, pull back the dust seal where the pushrod enters the cylinder to check for any seepage. If you notice fluid on the floor beneath the pedal, this is a sure sign of a leaking master cylinder. The 1275cc engine

Any sign of hydraulic fluid on the pedals or floor indicates a master cylinder leak. The rubber bung to the left of the clutch pedal provides access to the clutch slave cylinder bleed nipple on A-series versions. Ensure the pedal pivot bolt is tight and the pedals move without sideways free play.

versions incorporated a flexible hose between the solid pipe and slave cylinder which can also leak in time. It makes sense to replace this at the same time as replacing a slave cylinder, to ensure reliability of the hydraulic system. The Midget 1493cc engine can suffer excessively worn crankshaft thrust washers, and depressing the clutch pedal can simply drive the crankshaft forwards rather than releasing the clutch diaphragm unit.

2. Clutch release bearing

The 948cc, 1098cc and 1275cc engines used a non-rotating carbon graphite thrust release bearing; this can suffer a reduced life under heavy traffic driving conditions. Furthermore, some non-original specification release bearings may not be as durable as the original item. When worn, the bearing will not allow the clutch to disengage fully. Ordinarily, this will be a gradually worsening condition; however, it is not unknown for the bearing to break up

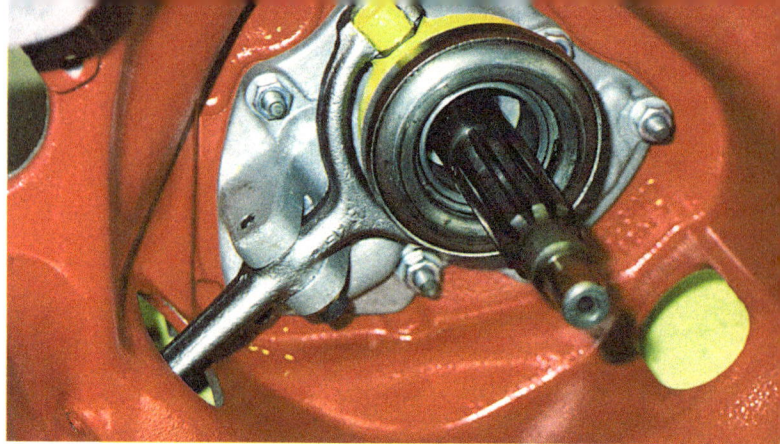

Peter May Engineering produces a ball bearing clutch release kit which does away with the carbon graphite bearing. It should prove both longer lasting and quieter in operation than the original.

suddenly making it impossible to disengage the clutch. A useful modification is available to replace the carbon graphite bearing with a ball bearing thrust race on a special bearing carrier. The mechanical components of the release mechanism should not be overlooked; accumulative wear in clevis pins and pivot holes can combine to make clutch disengagement difficult.

3. Clutch not engaging/slipping

Should the clutch only engage near the top of the pedal travel, or slip under heavy or sudden loading, it will need to be replaced. The clutch cannot be inspected externally, and must be removed from the car for examination. The engine must be removed, as it is not possible to remove the gearbox from underneath the car. The engine can either be removed singularly or with the gearbox as a complete unit.

The carbon graphite clutch release bearing. The one on the left is worn down to the steel housing. This is an early bearing for the spring clutch, whilst the part worn bearing on the right is for the 1275cc diaphragm clutch. Different housing – but it serves to demonstrate the amount of wear.

4. Clutch judder

Judder when engaging the clutch may be due to badly worn engine or gearbox rubber mountings. More likely, the clutch will be worn or contaminated with oil from an engine or gearbox leak. If the clutch is severely worn, the friction plate rivets may have scored the flywheel, necessitating this to be re-faced. A new clutch assembly will be required, which will comprise of the friction plate, cover unit and release bearing.

5. Clutch noise

A screeching sound when engaging the clutch may be heard with the 948cc, 1098cc and 1275cc engine versions. This is due to the non-rotating carbon graphite clutch release bearing contacting the rotating thrust pad on the clutch cover unit. With the 1275cc diaphragm clutch, the thrust pad can become loose within the spring fingers of the cover unit. This can cause noise and unevenness when the clutch pedal is depressed. A loud metallic screech is a sure sign that the release bearing and thrust pad are no longer a happy match. The 1493cc engine clutch may also produce some metallic noises if the release bearing fails, but this is less common. Any roughness or vibration felt when the pedal is depressed is an indication that the release bearing may be worn.

6. Gearchange problems

The gearchange on the early smooth casing gearboxes is rather spoilt by weak synchromesh, particularly on second gear which can become almost non-effective. The later ribbed case gearbox has much improved synchromesh, but still not on first gear. The gearchange quality may be further spoilt by not using the correct specification oil, which should be engine grade oil, not 80 grade oil which most other gearboxes are designed to use. This is a common error, as some owners deliberately use this thicker oil in an attempt to reduce the signs of wear and noise. It may be noticed that the gearlever pressure increases as the gearbox becomes hotter; a typical trait of these gearboxes. A badly worn gearbox may jump out of gear, and a rebuild will be the only cure. The 1493cc all synchromesh gearbox is generally very reliable, but can suffer from tired synchromesh after prolonged mileage. This gearbox requires 90 grade oil.

The 1275cc diaphragm clutch unit displaying a worn release bearing thrust face. This centrepiece can often become loose within the spring segments and create a screeching noise. Any roughness felt when depressing the clutch pedal indicates release bearing trouble.

The A-series gearbox oil filler plug is accessed through this aperture in the transmission tunnel. Be very careful not to cross thread the plug when refitting. The thread in the aluminium gearbox casing can very easily be damaged: do not over-tighten.

7. Gearbox noise

It is quite usual for the non-synchromesh first gear units to produce a noticeable whine when in this gear. Second and third gears may be slightly audible, but this should only be slight. Excessive noise, particularly a clanking or heavy rattling in first or reverse gears indicate worn layshaft bearings – this will require a complete gearbox rebuild. Noise transmitted through the gearlever may simply be the lever engaging with a worn plastic cup, or the anti-rattle spring and plunger. More likely however, it will be general accumulative wear throughout the gearbox. The Midget 1500 gearbox is generally fairly quiet but, again, noises can manifest after prolonged mileage which only a full overhaul will cure.

With the engine removed, the gearbox can be pulled forward with a trolley jack supporting the bellhousing. Oil will run out of the tail housing even though the drain plug is removed. Don't forget to release propshaft, gearlever, slave cylinder, speedo cable and reversing light cables first.

8. Driving sympathetically

With all versions, riding the clutch pedal or depressing the pedal for any longer than absolutely necessary should be avoided. Only engage first gear when you are ready to pull away, and always select neutral when stopped in traffic, with your foot away from the clutch pedal. This will preserve the life of the carbon release bearing on A-series versions, and the crankshaft thrust bearings on the Midget 1500.

A 6-gallon (27.3L) capacity pressed steel fuel tank is fitted below the boot floor. From GAN5-105501 the tank capacity was increased to 7 gallons (31.8L). Versions prior to HAN8/GAN3 were fitted with a mechanical engine-driven fuel pump mounted to the left-hand side of the engine. Subsequent versions used an SU electric pump mounted near to the right-hand rear shock absorber beneath the car. The 1493cc engine reverted to a mechanical engine-driven pump. All UK specification versions used a pair of SU carburettors, whilst the North American specification Midget 1500 used a single Zenith-Stromberg carburettor. In the course of production, three different sized SU carburettors were used, as follows:

Application	Type	Dia (in)
Sprite MkI (AN5)	SU H1	1.125
Sprite MkII to MkIV (HAN6 to AAN10)	SU HS2	1.250
Midget MkI to MkIII (GAN1 to GAN5)	SU HS2	1.250
Midget 1500 (GAN6)	SU HS4	1.5
Midget 1500 (North America)	Zenith-Stromberg	
(GAN6) Single carburettor	CD4 or CD4T	1.5

Externally, the various specifications of SU carburettors used look very much the same. However, many detail changes took place over the years. An identification tag on the float chamber lid will identify the exact specification and application when referring to the manufacturer's parts book.

Fuel

1. Fuel delivery problems

To start with the obvious, is there fuel in the tank? The fuel gauge may not be trustworthy, so do not assume that a reading is accurate. If the tank is old, then corrosion, sediment and other debris could restrict the fuel flow to the pump. The top of the tank is against the boot floor, and can rust away unseen – check for external leakage and the smell of fuel when the tank is full. The fuel filler cap is designed to act as the tank vent, except on North American versions from 1968. If replaced with a non-venting cap,

Twin SU HS4 carburettors were employed for the non-North American market Midget 1500. For North America, a single Zenith-Stromberg instrument was used to help clean exhaust emissions.

The lid being lifted on an SU electric fuel pump to reveal the contacts for the electromagnetic armature. The contacts do eventually fail but can be replaced.

No, not a coffee jar spillage. This is how much silt came out of one float chamber. Sediment build-up over the years can eventually upset clean running.

a vacuum may be formed in the tank as the fuel is drawn away. The vacuum can eventually overcome the fuel delivery and restrict or stop flow to the pump. Listen for air being drawn into the tank as you loosen the filler cap. A sucking noise will confirm that the tank is not being vented.

The SU fuel pump is usually reliable in regular usage, but can fail following a long period of idleness or infrequent use. Many owners fit a more modern type of pump to improve reliability. The SU pump can be heard operating as a muffled clunking sound from the right-hand rear side of the car. Mechanical pumps are generally reliable, but over a prolonged period may suffer leakage, failing non-return valves and a perished pump diaphragm. To ensure that small particles of sediment or debris do not reach the float chamber needle valves and cause flooding, many owners fit an in-line fuel filter near to the carburettors. This also gives a visible indication through the clear plastic body of the

Splits in the fuel hose, this obvious, are highly dangerous. It's very important to only use the correct grade fuel hose when replacing.

filter that the fuel pump is working. Otherwise, to check for fuel flow, disconnect the pipe to the carburettor, but be very aware that fuel will spurt out over the engine if the pump is working. Be prepared to catch spilt fuel safely. An electric pump will operate when the ignition is turned on. Early mechanical pumps have a hand-priming lever. The Midget 1500 pump will operate when the engine is turned over by the starter motor, so disconnect the ignition supply to prevent the engine from starting.

2. Fuel tank

The larger 7-gallon (31.8L) fuel tank can be used as a replacement for the original tank, offering a useful increase in range. The larger, deeper tank can be fitted to earlier versions, but be aware that the fuel level sender unit may need to be changed to suit. The Sprite MkI tank used a longer, integral fuel filler neck without an interconnecting sleeve as on later versions. A later type tank can be fitted to the MkI using a suitable sleeve, and the original MkI filler neck sawn off the original tank. Needless to say, remove all possibilities of igniting any fuel vapour if doing this. North American fuel tanks have a separate breather pipe connection after 1968, this being located adjacent to the filler hole. The fuel tank for the North American Midget 1500 has a capacity limiting chamber which reduced content by around 4 pints (2.3L). For unleaded fuel, a modified filler neck with a flap allowed only the unleaded fuel pump filler nozzle to be used. The fuel gauge float sensor is mounted in the top face of the tank. If the gauge fails or gives an inaccurate reading, the tank will need to be dropped to gain access to the sender unit.

3. Fuel leakage

Given time, a fuel leak can develop from almost any part of the fuel system. Always be vigilant, check regularly for signs of fuel

Should the float chamber overfill, fuel will spill out from the vent hole hidden under this cover, below the fuel pipe connection. From 1968, North American regulations demanded that all expelled vapours and fluids be connected to the emissions control circuit. Venting any vapour or spillage to atmosphere is now illegal. Remember, the exhaust manifold is just below the carburettors! If you smell fuel, investigate immediately.

smell and leakage, and investigate cause immediately. There are several pipe connections between tank, fuel pump and twin carburettors. Over time, these can perish, corrode or loosen. The float chamber needle valve is a common item to fail, allowing the float chamber to overfill and leak via the vent hole just below the delivery hose connection. Any dampness on the lid of the float chamber is a sure sign of this. Also, a punctured plastic float, or

the end of the delivery pipe leaking may be the culprit. There is a small flexible pipe between the bottom of the float chamber and carburettor jet assembly on the HS2 and HS4 types which can leak, especially from the float chamber end.

4. Carburettor backfire/spitback
This can be caused by one or more inlet valves not seating properly, incorrect ignition timing, or the HT leads not being re-fitted in the correct order. It is always a good idea to number the HT leads if you are uncertain as to the correct connection to each sparkplug.

5. Idle speed
The idle speed is set by the throttle stop screws on each carburettor; the speed being between 800 to 950rpm dependant upon the engine. A modified engine may have a considerably higher and uneven idle speed if a camshaft with greater overlap and valve lift is fitted. Once set, the throttle stop screws should not need to be reset. However, if the idle speed should alter or become uneven in service, check the following:
• The contact breaker gap and ignition timing are correct.
• Sparkplugs and HT circuit are good.
• The compression pressure is correct.
• Check for air leakage in the induction system, including worn throttle spindles.
• The choke is operating and releasing fully.
• The carburettor dashpot pistons are operating freely.
• Float chambers are not flooding.
• The main jets and metering needles are centred properly and not worn.
• Check also that the throttle cable is not sticking, and the throttle return springs have not become detached or slackened.

The main components to renew when overhauling a carburettor: the throttle spindle, metering needle, fuel jet and the float chamber needle valve assembly. The new jet must be centralised properly to the tapered metering needle.

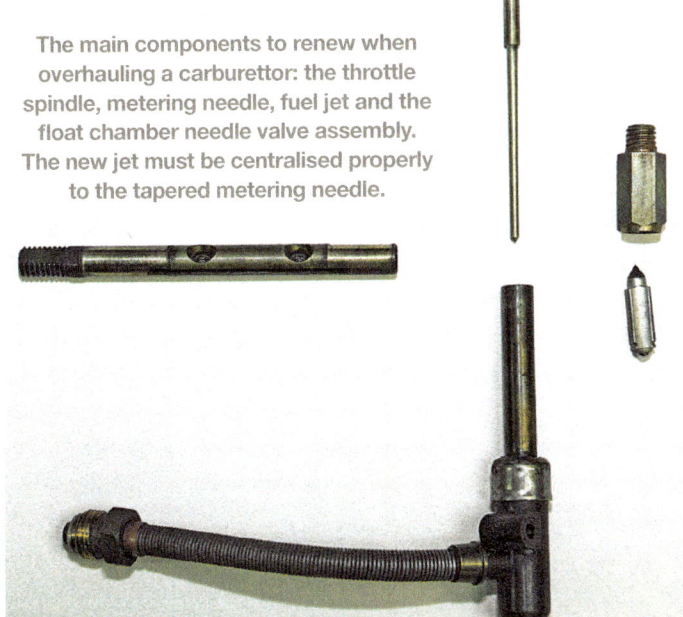

The dashpot and piston assembly with control spring and damper above. The piston must be a good sliding fit in the dashpot. Handle with great care to ensure that the metering needle is not bent. Various control springs are used, depending on engine spec. Ensure you have a matched pair suitable for your particular version.

both the metering needle and jet is vital to ensure the correct fuel/air ratio is maintained throughout the engine's operating range. Any wear will result in poor performance, uneven running and increased fuel consumption.

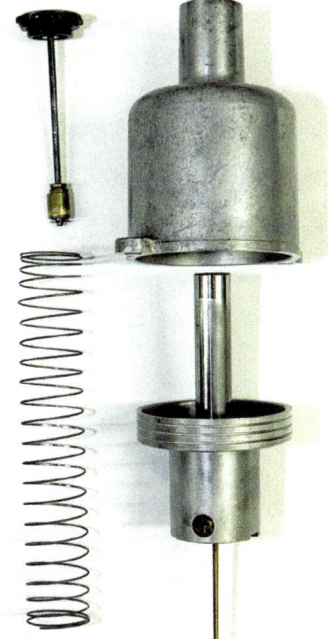

6. Main jet centering

It is important that the jet tube is set centrally to the metering needle, so that the brass needle will not bind or suffer premature wear by rubbing in the jet. Remove the dashpot damper piston, and use the dashpot piston lifting pin to raise the piston. On releasing the pin, the piston should drop immediately with a solid sound as it drops onto the stop. If not, it's possible that the needle is either rubbing in the jet, or the piston is sticking in the dashpot. Later in production, a spring-loaded self-centring needle was introduced to overcome this problem. The good condition of

7. Carburettor wear

Unless the carburettors are in good condition, the engine will never perform as intended. There are a few basic checks that should be made when investigating poor starting or running. The throttle spindle, which passes through the carburettor body, can wear sufficiently to allow air to be drawn into the carburettor venturi. This will upset the fuel to air ratio over the operating range and make the correct tuning of the carburettors impossible. To check, grasp the end of the throttle spindle, just where it enters the body, and try moving the spindle up and down. Any

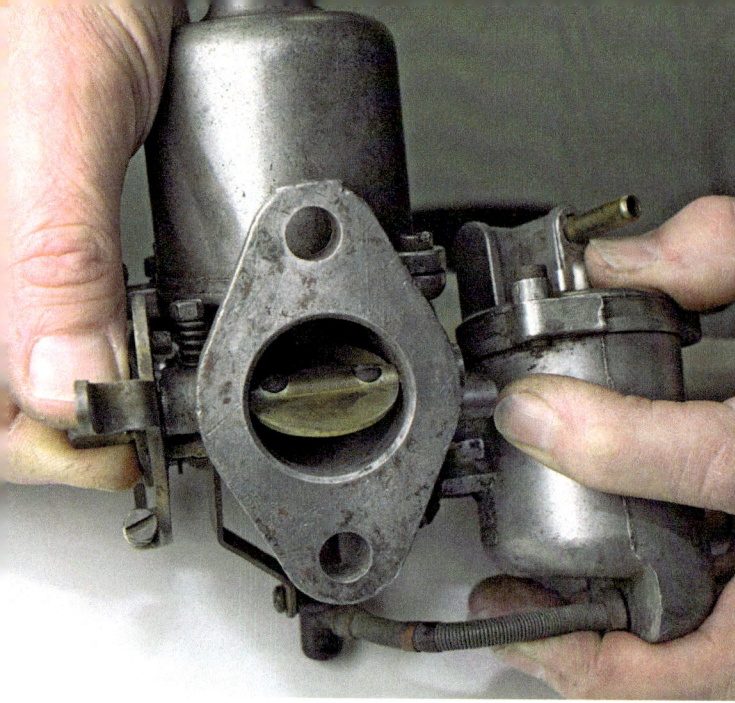

With the throttle open, check for vertical and lateral movement at the end of the spindle. Replacing the spindle is usually sufficient; the alloy body rarely wears significantly.

the correct rate. Any sticking will upset the running. The piston is controlled by a spring and a hydraulic damper. The oil level within the damper, at the top of the dashpot, must be maintained at the correct level. I always use engine oil, as thinner type oils soon disappear. The balance between the two carburettors must be set correctly for airflow, mixture strength and idle speed.

8. Zenith-Stromberg carburettor

Fitted only to the North American Midget 1500 as a single unit, this is very similar in operation to the SU. Here, the dashpot piston is controlled by a flexible diaphragm. In time, the diaphragm can split, seriously upsetting the running of the engine. Place this high on your list of things to check should the engine start misbehaving. The Zenith-Stromberg 150 CD4 carburettor was replaced by the 150 CD4T from GAN6-UG-166304 (October 1975), this being basically the same but now with an automatic choke. Poor starting may be due to malfunctioning of the automatic choke.

9. Induction air leaks

In addition to air being drawn in through worn throttle spindles, check the following items if the correct fuel air mixture cannot be maintained:
• The vacuum advance pipe from one carburettor to the vacuum advance diaphragm unit on the distributor.
• The closed circuit crankcase ventilation pipework and connections.
• From March 1964 to May 1968, a 'Smiths' diaphragm valve, mounted on the inlet manifold controlled the recirculation of crankcase fumes. The rubber diaphragm could fail allowing manifold depression to draw excess air and oil fumes into the combustion chambers via the inlet manifold. Not only is

movement other than rotational indicates that the carburettor needs to be reconditioned. In most instances, just a new brass spindle will be required for each carburettor. It's rare for the alloy body to wear significantly enough that bushes need to be fitted. Usually, the brass spindle wears at a much faster rate than the alloy body. The dashpot piston must rise and fall smoothly and at

In addition to checking the Smiths valve for leakage, check the tightness of the manifold nuts and the vacuum advance pipe to the distributor. Note the original air filter casings containing replaceable paper element filters. Don't forget to check these for cleanliness. The oil filler cap contains a breather; this should be replaced periodically.

The Smiths valve was replaced by a 'Y' piece venting directly into each carburettor body. This proved a more reliable system. As before, check the condition of all pipework and connections, as leakage will cause poor running and allow the escape of oil fumes.

performance compromised, but the amount of blue smoke from the exhaust can look like a far more serious engine problem. This system was replaced by venting directly into each carburettor body via a 'Y' piece. This has proven far more reliable but again, the condition of the hoses and connections must be examined and replaced if at all doubtful.

• Check the carburettor flange nuts for tightness. The sandwich of heat insulation block and heatshield requires three gaskets

between each carburettor and manifold, and each face must be airtight. The manifold nuts should also be checked, as these do loosen following a manifold gasket replacement and may allow air to be drawn in.

• If a brake servo has been fitted, check the connection and hose to this. The servo could have an internal air leak if the main diaphragm is breaking up. From 1968, versions for the North American market had to comply with new emissions control regulations. This added more pipework to the induction system and more items to check for possible air leakage. When fitted, the correct operation of the anti-run-on valve should be checked. Should this stick open, the engine will draw excessive air and not start.

10. Air filters

One of the most common modifications is to fit a different type of air filter. Some are very good; others less so. In all cases, check that a non-original air filter does not block the dashpot vent hole in the mounting flange on the carburettor body. Fitting the standard air filter backplate upside down will also block the vent hole, thereby affecting the correct operation

Whatever type of air filter is used, ensure that the dashpot vent hole is not blocked by the filter backing plate. Be careful not to damage the mounting hole threads in the soft alloy casting.

of the dashpot piston. Always use care when removing or refitting the air filter backplate – the threads in the carburettor mounting flange can easily be damaged. Once a thread in the soft alloy has been stripped, either repair with a 'Helicoil' insert or, by using a longer bolt, a nut can just about be used on the opposite side of the mounting face. An engine should not be operated without an efficient or effective air filter. Ingested particles or foreign objects can accelerate wear or cause serious internal damage.

11. Vaporisation

The twin carburettors are provided with heat insulation blocks and a heatshield to protect from heat transfer. However, under very hot conditions, the fuel in the float chambers and feed pipes can vaporise, causing hot starting problems or lack of power. This can be exacerbated on modified examples, where the heatshield has been left off or cut away to allow the fitting of certain tubular-type exhaust manifolds or different carburettors. The electric SU fuel pump may be heard operating continuously when vaporising occurs. Tubular exhaust manifolds can be wrapped in a special heat insulation tape to reduce under bonnet heat build-up.

12. Carburettor controls

In time, the bottom hinge of the organ-type throttle pedal can become stiff, and even seize. Once seized, the hinge can then break, making precise throttle control rather difficult. Some owners simply remove the pedal and drive with their foot on the throttle bar. An occasional squirt of oil on the pedal hinge is a good preventive. The Midget 1500 used a pendant pedal which avoided this problem. The throttle action should be very smooth on the earlier versions, but due to the design of the linkage on the Midget 1500, can be stiff and imprecise. Throttle cables rarely break, other than perhaps with the 1500 engine, or possibly with

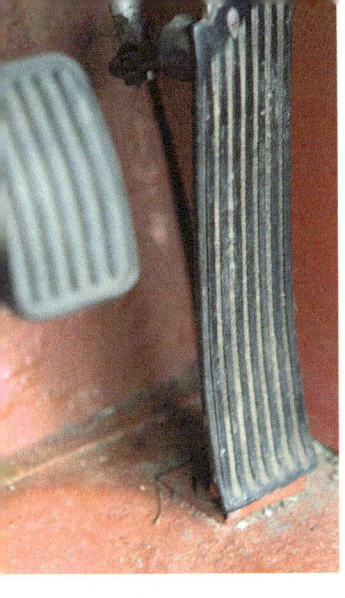

Pre-Midget 1500 versions all used a lower hinged throttle pedal. The hinge can seize and break if neglected under a sodden carpet. A drop of oil now and again should maintain perfect throttle control.

The Midget 1500 throttle linkage can be stiff and imprecise. Here, the owner has modified the linkage by extending the vertical link to improve the operating geometry.

Cold start fuel management system. A clothes peg is a familiar item to hold open a non-locking choke control or a locking choke that has lost this feature. Here, we see summer and winter setting pieces!

a change to a non-original type of induction system. Always exercise care when removing or replacing the throttle and choke cables. The anchorage ends can easily be frayed when passing through the cable anchors. Once frayed, they can be very difficult to feed through the anchors, and may bind or become stuck in the outer cable in use. Check the cable and replace if any strands are breaking free or missing. Ensure that the choke operates correctly. When fully pulled out, check that the SU jet tubes are drawn down from both carburettor bodies fully. If the jet tubes move unevenly or only partly, then starting from cold may prove difficult. It is important that the choke mechanism is correctly adjusted to allow both throttle spindles to be rotated slightly to the fast idle speed setting. The A-series engine heatshield anchors the throttle return springs, check that these are present and correctly attached. In time, a fracture may develop across the heatshield due to the force of the springs pulling on the bottom edge. The shield for the 1275cc engine had the addition of two support brackets; these braced the lower edge from the engine. This is a good modification to make to the earlier versions, thus preventing the shield from breaking and losing the throttle return spring tension, probably when you'd least expect it.

13. Unleaded fuel.
Only the North American Midget 1500 was equipped to run on unleaded fuel with the fitment of specially hardened valve seat inserts. To run on unleaded fuel on all other versions, either the cylinder head must be similarly modified, or a suitable fuel additive used. If choosing the latter, be aware that different additives may have a different chemical base and should not be mixed or interchanged. When selecting which additive to use, choose wisely and stick to it.

14. Emissions equipment
From 1968, North American regulations regarding emissions from vehicles meant that Spridgets bound for that market had to incorporate additional features. These became even more stringent as the years progressed, but essentially these were introduced to prevent any fluid or venting of fumes direct to atmosphere. Hence, all crankcase venting was re-circulated through the combustion chambers or to carbon absorption canisters. Fuel venting was similarly vented from the float chambers and fuel tank through a closed absorption system before reaching atmosphere. This all meant a lot more pipework, connections and components in the system, all of which required periodic inspection and servicing as required. Some owners may be tempted to remove or reduce the items of emissions control equipment, but must be aware that this may infringe local regulations.

Exhaust system
All versions employed a cast iron exhaust manifold and mild steel exhaust system. Early versions had a single, rear-mounted silencer box, but from October 1969, a secondary transversely mounted box was added. From March 1975, for California, and from October 1975 for the rest of North America, the Midget 1500 was fitted with a catalytic convertor just below the exhaust manifold.

1. Common problems
Being mild steel, the exhaust system will have a limited life due to corrosion. This is particularly evident in the silencer box. The bottom of the box will corrode through first. Initially, this may go unnoticed as gas leakage noise may only be very slight. The transverse secondary silencer is more prone to corrosion

The bracket between the bellhousing and exhaust downpipe is essential to prevent the torque reaction of the engine acting against the exhaust system. The bracket is vulnerable to damage, being the lowest part of the car. A non-original tubular steel manifold is seen here; some adaption may be needed if using different manifolds. Without the bracket, tubular steel manifolds will be strained as the engine rocks in use.

restricting gas flow. Mountings may become detached, or indeed, the complete system left behind. Always check the system if the car has grounded at any time. Stainless steel exhaust systems are available for all versions and make a sensible choice when replacing.

2. Manifold

The manifold to downpipe joint, on earlier versions, consisted of a tapered bell mouth and clamp. This can prove very temperamental in maintaining a good seal, especially if the torque reaction bracket between the downpipe to bellhousing is not fitted correctly. It is not unknown for the cast iron manifold to crack at this joint, when the clamp has been continually over-tightened to attempt to make a seal. From November 1967, North American specification manifolds were fitted with a flange fitting to a revised downpipe, which provided a much more reliable joint. Home market Midgets had to wait until August 1973 to receive this type of manifold. Many owners have fitted a tubular steel exhaust manifold as a replacement to cure this problem, and as a performance upgrade. However, these manifolds can produce their own problems. Often, the carburettor heatshield has to be modified or removed, and the aperture in the frame modified to allow adequate clearances for the two pipes of the manifold. Even so, some manifolds may rattle against the surrounding metal if adequate clearance has not been achieved. Being mild steel, tubular manifolds can still corrode in time and develop stress cracks.

damage – this is caused by the cooler and condensing water content of the exhaust gas passing through and leaving residue in the box. This prompts many owners to retro fit the earlier single box system, generally being cheaper, longer lasting and, very importantly, sounding more sporty. Being so close to the road surface, the system is vulnerable to damage from present day speed bumps or other hazards and road debris. The effective pipe diameter may become reduced by impact damage, thereby

The screwdriver indicates where early cast iron exhaust manifolds can crack if the clamp is over-tightened or the torque reaction bracket is missing. Both solid cast and pressed steel clamps are available.

3. Emissions control

From 1968, versions for the North American market were equipped with a belt-driven air injection pump. This admitted air into the exhaust ports through tapings in a modified cylinder head casting. The condition of the pump, pipework and injectors on these versions must be checked to ensure that exhaust gas emissions are not compromised. Some owners remove the pump and fit blanks into the injector holes to improve performance and simplify the engine ancillaries. However, this practice may infringe local emissions regulations. The Midget 1500 for North America was equipped with an exhaust gas recirculation valve (EGRV) from a taping in the manifold. Again, the correct operation of this must be ensured. Initially, the catalytic convertor below the exhaust manifold required a service change at 25,000-mile intervals. A service indicator was incorporated with the EGRV indicator for this reason. From GAN6-212000 (May 1978), the indicator only provided the EGRV function.

Another tubular steel manifold, this one wrapped in heat insulating tape to prevent the radiating heat reaching the single SU HIF carburettor. This non-original combination has done away with the standard pressed steel heatshield. This type of manifold, also known as an LCB (long centre branch), requires extra clearance through the splash shield between the frame rails at the bottom of the engine compartment. Some types can be a very tight fit and may rattle against the frame rails. A hammer seems to be favourite to cure this!

All UK market versions used a Lucas-supplied ignition system, utilising a traditional coil and distributor with contact breaker points and condenser. Timing on these versions is controlled by centrifugal weights within the distributor body and

Externally, Lucas distributors can look very much alike. Internally, the amount and rate of ignition advance is preset to suit the specific application for which it is intended. An identification number stamped on the side of the body can be used to determine the correct application when referring to the manufacturer's reference list.

vacuum advance economy connection from the carburettor. Prior to the 1493cc engine, the coil was provided with a constant 12 volt feed from the ignition switch. The Midget 1500 had a dual input voltage coil to provide a stronger high tension output for starting, a ballast resistor reducing the feed voltage for normal running. An amplifier was introduced to the distributor for North American Midgets from October 1975. It should be stressed that, externally, the distributors used all look very similar. However, the internal specification with regard to the rate and amount of ignition advance changed several times over the period of production. An identification number is stamped on the distributor body as a reference to the correct application. Ensure that the correct distributor is fitted or performance will suffer.

Common problems

For the engine to start promptly and perform correctly, the ignition system must be maintained in good order. Even so, faults may occur in service which will demand immediate attention. Your workshop manual will explain the more usual service topics, so here we will take a more in depth look at the things which can cause problems.

1. Distributor bearing wear

The centre shaft bearing will suffer wear over prolonged mileage. The shaft will then develop a sideways movement, creating an inconsistent contact breaker gap and dwell angle. Not only will this make setting the contact breaker gap inaccurate, but the varying gap when running can cause ignition timing and voltage

With the rotor arm fitted, turn against the direction of rotation, and the shaft should spring back when released. If not, then either the upper part of the shaft is seized to the lower shaft or the centrifugal weight springs have become inoperative. Any of these faults will necessitate a reconditioned distributor.

2. Distributor low tension circuit

Check the internal low tension cables, these are often overlooked and can break when replacing the contact breaker points. A new set of contact points will usually need re-setting after a few hundred miles. The heel of the cam follower will wear into the profile and angle of the cam, reducing the points gap quite considerably. Don't forget to use a small amount of grease on the follower to lubricate it, and a drop of engine oil in the top of the shaft beneath the rotor arm. If the faces of the contact points are very badly burnt, it could indicate that the condenser needs replacing. Pay particular attention to the removal and refitting order of the contact points. It is very easy to get this wrong, with the result that the engine will not start. The low tension cables to the condenser and external connector must be touching the contact breaker spring, and they must not be fitted on top of the insulator bush. There have been some quality issues with currently remanufactured ignition components, condensers and contact points, and rotor arms have failed prematurely in some instances. Wise to carry a spare of each.

Check for bearing wear by attempting to rock the shaft sideways. Lateral movement will mean a replacement distributor is required. The amount of ignition advance in degrees is stamped on the centrifugal weight plate.

fluctuations. Try moving the shaft at right angles to the axis, if any movement is felt then the top bearing is worn. You may find that the contact breaker gap is different at each peak of the cam lobe.

3. Distributor high tension circuit

A small hairline crack in the distributor cap, which may be almost invisible to the naked eye, will almost certainly manifest itself through difficult starting in damp conditions. The rotor arm is normally reliable, but check for burning at the tip and on the corresponding brass contacts within the cap. Some replacement rotor arms have been of poor quality, so may not last for very long, and might be faulty from the start. The spring-loaded carbon contact in the centre of the cap should not be overlooked – check for wear, damage and freedom of movement against the spring. If damp start performance is poor, try observing the distributor and HT leads in the

Check the contact breaker gap at the peak of each cam lobe to ensure that it is constant. If not, either the bearings are worn or the shaft is bent and the unit should be replaced. A new contact breaker set will need to be re-checked after a few hundred miles, as the cam follower heel can wear down quite rapidly until properly bedded into the cam lobe profile.

Check the four contacts for burning and signs of cracks in the cap. Ensure the spring-loaded centre brush is in good condition and moving freely.

dark; you may see the HT current tracking around the distributor and leads as the engine is motored on the starter. You may also hear a cracking sound as the HT voltage arcs to earth. A set of new HT leads, distributor cap, rotor arm and sparkplug caps are not expensive items, and well worth replacing or keeping to hand in your emergency spares box.

4. Sparkplugs

It is important to use the correct heat grade sparkplugs for your engine, (details in the workshop manual). For engines which have been modified, a different grade of sparkplug may be required. You might need expert advice to determine which grade of plug best suits your engine. The colour of combustion deposits on the sparkplug gives a good indication of the health of the engine. Importantly, deposits on each plug should be the same colour. Any variations will indicate that combustion within a cylinder is out of balance with the others. This fault may result from a number of causes, including loss of compression from valve seating problems, piston ring blow past, cylinder head leakage, carburettor imbalance, or an ignition HT fault. Please refer to the appropriate chapter for more on this. It should be noted that engines using a fuel additive to protect against valve seat recession may produce a variation of colouring dependant upon their chemical base. Nevertheless, each sparkplug should still have an even colouring.

5. Coil and external wiring

Check the wiring and connections to the coil and distributor – these can become corroded and break off with the movement of the engine. The low tension terminals are secured with a nut on early examples, but riveted on later examples. The rivets can loosen and the spade terminals develop cracks. The coil is generally very reliable, but should an engine develop a tendency to cut out when hot, then the coil could be at fault. If the engine re-starts when cooled, this may well be the culprit. The coil can be checked by disconnecting the LT leads and placing a multimeter across the LT connections on the coil. A 12-volt-fed coil should produce around a 3 ohm resistance, whilst the ballast resistor-fed coil should be around 1.6 ohms. To check the HT winding in the coil, make a connection from the CB, or minus, connection to the central HT outlet, this should indicate a 7 kohm to 10 kohm resistance. If the polarity of the electrical system has been changed, the coil low tension connections should be swapped. Positive earth coil LT terminals are marked CB (contact breaker) and SW (secondary winding) and negative earth coils marked – (contact breaker) and + (secondary winding). Other than the LT terminal markings, the two types of coil are identical and can be swapped provided that the correct wiring connections are made. The dual voltage cold start coil must not be used without the ballast resistor, to reduce feed voltage for normal running. Fitting a cold start coil to a pre-Midget 1500 version will overheat the coil with eventual failure. When checking the feed from the ignition switch to the coil, the Midget 1500 must be checked with the ignition key in both the start and then running positions.

6. Electronic ignition

Although not fitted originally, some owners have fitted aftermarket electronic ignition systems to solve problems or to improve performance. Some earlier types have proved more problematic than the original system. You can now fit an electronic system within the original distributor body to retain original appearance. If you are unfamiliar with your car, you could find that any undeclared modifications leave you scratching your head should a problem arise. Some owners carry an original distributor and ignition system as a back up to a modified system, just in case of such a problem. Generally, electronic systems are now much more reliable than they used to be, provided they are fitted correctly.

7. Starting problem checklist

• Using a multimeter, check the supply to the coil with the ignition turned on. This will be to the SW low tension terminal for positive earth, and + terminal for negative earth. If a positive earth system has been converted to negative earth, then the coil terminal connections should have been swapped over at the same time. Although the coil will still function if the polarity is incorrect, it will not deliver full performance. For the Midget 1500 with a dual voltage input coil, check the input voltage with the ignition switch in the start position – the supply voltage should be 12V, and then in the run position, when the voltage should drop to around 7V.

• With the distributor cap removed, check the gap of the contact breaker and condition of the faces. If incorrect or badly burnt, either reface, or replace to the correct setting. Turn the engine so the contact breaker is closed and, with the ignition switched on, flick open the contacts with a small screwdriver. You should see a spark and hear a click. If not, investigate the low tension circuit to the distributor. Check the CB or – (negative) cable from the coil to the distributor and the small LT cables within the distributor body.

• Check the spring-loaded carbon brush contact in the distributor cap and the four brass contact points feeding the HT lead.

Check the rotor arm and cap for any signs of cracking, tracking or contamination from oil or moisture. Check the HT leads and each plug cap. Don't forget the HT lead to the coil. Remove this from the coil to check that the connection is sound and dry. With the plugs removed and the ignition on, spin the engine over and check for a spark at each plug electrode gap. A warning here: keep the plugs well away from the sparkplug holes, since any fuel vapour being expelled from the sparkplug holes may find the spark. You do not want to experience an external combustion if you value your eyebrows!

8. Running-on

An engine that will not immediately cease firing when the ignition is turned off is termed as *running-on*. This is due to excessive combustion chamber temperature causing the fuel/air mix to detonate through heat, rather than by a spark from the sparking plug. Possible causes include overheating (an excessive carbon build-up promoting localised hot spots), over advanced ignition timing, too high an idling speed, or a very high compression ratio. Too low a fuel octane content may also promote this fault. Many production engines can suffer this malady without actually having a definitive fault, resulting more from the combination of basic design and prevailing running conditions. The North American Midget 1500 is fitted with an anti-run-on valve (AROV) as standard to guard against this. When the ignition is switched off, the valve opens to admit air into the inlet manifold and destroy the induction vacuum. An AROV can be fitted to other engines, with a little modification, should running-on be a persistent problem without any obvious causes.

A vertical flow radiator, provided with a pressure cap of 7lb/in^2 was used until 1968. This was replaced by a smaller crossflow radiator with separate expansion tank and a pressure cap of 15lb/in^2. An engine-driven fan with fixed blades provided the cooling draught. A thermostat in the cylinder head controlled operating temperature with an engine-driven water pump providing circulation.

1. Coolant leaks

A loss of coolant should be investigated immediately. This may be an obvious leak from a hose, connection, radiator or a core plug in the cylinder block. Minor leaks will leave tell-tale staining.

The crossflow radiator had a separate expansion tank with a higher pressure cap. Check the tank and interconnecting pipe for signs of leakage.

Pressure changes in the top tank of the early vertical flow radiator can cause stress cracks to form. The number of reinforcement flutes was increased from three to four on later examples, which helped to stiffen the area.

Leakage in the heater matrix may be more difficult to detect (if the windscreen becomes misted up for no apparent reason, with a tell-tale smell of hot coolant, then this may be the cause). The water pump can leak from around the spindle; this is not always easy to see until it becomes more serious. Try moving the fan blades backwards and forwards to see if there is any play in the spindle bearings. There should be no perceptible movement at all. The

The heater tap on all versions can develop a leak: check for staining around the valve, and the condition of the adjoining hose and clip.

The A-series water pumps. A non-original alloy-bodied pump (below) can suffer severe alloy corrosion. Both the bottom hose stub and bypass hose stub can dissolve away in time. The original cast iron-bodied pump (upper) has a steel tube insert for the bypass hose, this too can suffer severe corrosion. Look for signs of coolant leakage from the hole beneath the pump nose.

A-series engines have a thermostat bypass hose between the water pump and cylinder head. Leaks can develop here and may be difficult spot until serious, so check this area carefully and regularly. To replace the hose, either the cylinder head or water pump must be removed or a special thin-walled convoluted hose used. This can be squeezed into place after cutting out the faulty hose with a knife. It should be noted that the convoluted hose is a quick fix repair, and unlikely to last as long as the proper thick-walled water hose. Both the water pump and cylinder head stub tubes can corrode sufficiently to prevent a water-tight seal. Some replacement water pumps seem to be made of an inferior quality alloy and can corrode quite badly. This can be serious enough for the bottom hose stub to crumble away. Always use the correct mix of good quality antifreeze or corrosion inhibitor to protect against corrosion damage as well as ice formation. Although most coolant loss will be apparent externally, a leaking cylinder head gasket may be more difficult to trace. A slight leakage into a cylinder or pushrod hole may not be immediately obvious. If a coolant loss cannot be found externally, then a compression test or coolant contamination test should be carried out. A more severe gasket leakage can produce white smoke from the exhaust, a loss of power, overheating, water contamination of the lubricating oil and coolant being ejected from the radiator overflow pipe. The formation of 'mayonnaise,' a creamy semi-fluid gunge on the inside of the rocker cover and oil filler cap, can be a sign of coolant getting into the lubrication system. However, this can also be caused by frequent low temperature running, or partially blocked or ineffective crankcase ventilation system.

2. Overheating

All versions can run at a higher than normal water temperature under arduous driving conditions. The water temperature gauge

The thermostat is more likely to fail in the open position. It can, however, stick shut if left for a prolonged period. Keep a careful watch on the temperature gauge. The A-series thermostat housing may need some persuasion to release from the cylinder head.

needs to be watched under such conditions. However, the temperature should return to normal afterwards. A sustained high temperature may indicate a cooling system deficiency, such as poor water circulation, insufficient airflow through the radiator, a sticking thermostat, low coolant level or a leaking cylinder head gasket. Various temperature rated thermostats are available, so you can experiment a little to suit your particular example if modified or driven hard. Many owners fit an electric

Check for signs of leakage on the bypass hose between cylinder head and water pump. The convoluted 'thin-walled' hose should be treated as an emergency repair only. Always use a thick-walled hose as here. Note the alloy corrosion on the water pump and where the thermostat housing has been removed.

engine cooling fan in front of the radiator to either supplement or replace the engine-driven fan. Check that this electric fan is operating correctly and blowing cooling air in the right direction.

Ensure you have the correct fan for the application, that it is fitted properly and cutting in at the appropriate temperature. If the thermostat is removed from the system, the coolant will not circulate around the rear of the engine sufficiently and this can cause localised overheating around the rear cylinders. Sediment build-up in the cylinder block and radiator can restrict circulation. This sediment can be removed with proprietary cooling system flushing compounds but, if excessive, a replacement radiator and removal of the core plugs for a thorough clean of the block may be necessary.

A low coolant level may manifest itself with a high temperature gauge reading, but with no heat available from the heater. The heater matrix is placed at the highest point in the system and will drain as coolant is lost.

Poor air circulation through the radiator matrix can be caused by a build-up of debris becoming lodged in the matrix. This is usually airborne insects, grass, straw, mud, or any other item that road conditions may throw into the front of your car. Check the state of the matrix through the radiator grille regularly, and clean out as necessary. Remember, if you fit extra driving lights, a badge bar, rally plate or any other item in front of the radiator, airflow may be impeded.

3. Over cooling

An engine that fails to reach normal operating temperature should be investigated. Firstly, ensure that the temperature gauge is working correctly. A secondary test gauge may be required to check this out. Most likely, the thermostat located at the front of the cylinder head has failed. The alloy thermostat housing can corrode, and seize on the securing studs. Be aware that you may need to replace the housing if it has not been disturbed for many years, because you may have to destroy it to remove it. It's

best to replace the steel studs with stainless steel bolts; also use some copper grease on reassembly. Various thermostat opening temperature ratings are available, so ensure that you select the correct thermostat for your model. If the old thermostat is partly open when you remove it, this is a sure sign that it has failed. If an electric engine cooling fan has been fitted, is this running too often? The thermostatic control switch may not be set correctly or has stuck in the 'on' position.

4. Water pump

Over tensioning of the drivebelt will put extra strain on the water pump bearings and may reduce bearing life. Similarly, the dynamo or alternator bearings will suffer. The original pump body for the A-series engines was made of cast iron with a screwed in steel stub for the by-pass hose connection. Over time, the stub

The alloy thermostat housing can corrode badly; this one was caught before the top hose was blown off. Beware a slight coolant leak; it could very soon become serious.

Compare the depth of the water pump impeller of the non-original pump (left) to the original version (right). The deep impeller can contact No 1 cylinder casting on the 1275cc engine and jamb. Check that the pump spindle is free to turn before replacing anything else.

can corrode sufficiently to cause coolant leakage. Replacement pumps are available from a number of manufacturers, but now with an alloy casting and varying impeller designs. Some impellers are much deeper and can come into contact with number 1 cylinder casting in certain instances. When fitting a new pump, check that the spindle will rotate freely before tightening the retaining screws. If the impeller is contacting the cylinder wall casting, obtain a pump of different manufacture.

5. Oil cooling

An oil cooler became a factory-fitted option to address a significant reduction of oil pressure under hot and hard driving conditions. The cooler was fitted in front of the water radiator, with a hose leading from the rear of the A-series engine block to the cooler, and returning via a second hose to the oil filter adaptor head. The condition of these hoses needs to be checked, along with the cooler matrix, for any signs of damage and leakage. The factory-fitted oil cooler came with a blanking plate for use in cold weather conditions, so as not to over cool the oil. Present day oil cooler kits may include a thermostatic valve to bypass the cooler until the oil reaches a pre-determined temperature. It is not good for an engine to run with oil at too low a temperature.

6. Coolant

It is important to use antifreeze, not only to protect from freezing, but to inhibit the cooling system against corrosion and blockage. Use antifreeze in the correct ratio, according to the information

The early-type heater unit with separate blower fan. Check for green staining on the brass body of the heater tap. The short 'U'-shaped hose has to absorb the movement between the engine and heater unit; check for cracking.

supplied. There are also other coolant additives available which claim to prevent cavitation within the system, and protect against corrosive attack. There are sealants which can reduce or stop some forms of leakage, but do not over use such products. They should be just a temporary cure until the fault can be properly repaired.

7. Ineffective heater

Two types of Smiths heater were used. Early versions had a separate single speed blower fan mounted before the heater box. From 1970, a larger box contained the flap valve, blower and matrix. The later type was claimed to have a higher output, but both should prove to be quite effective. The most common reasons for loss of heater output are as follows:

• Low coolant temperature due to faulty thermostat.
• Heater tap not fully turned on or stuck.
• Restriction within the matrix; this can be in the heater, water or airflow passages.
• Main air duct flap valve not opening.
• Blower motor not working; often due to dashboard switch not functioning.

It is quite straightforward to remove the heater unit from the car. Release the clips holding the box together and then remove the matrix for inspection. The combined air flap and blower motor control can fail, so check that both functions are operating correctly. Check that the main air ducting tube to the front of the car is in good order; if this is split, engine smells can reach the interior.

Inspecting the heater matrix for leakage is not made easy by it being contained within a steel box. If the windscreen tends to mist up when the heater is on, plus there's a smell of hot coolant, suspect a leaking matrix.

The front suspension is provided by a coil spring acting upon a pressed steel wishbone. The stub axle pivots about a vertical kingpin, with a lever arm shock absorber acting as the upper link. A swivel trunnion block fitted with two metalastic bushes provides the pivot between the kingpin and lever arm. Steering is by way of a rack and pinion unit mounted ahead of the front wheel axis. A front anti-roll bar became a standard fitment for home market versions from GAN5-138801 (August 1973) but remained an option elsewhere. Each stub axle was provided with two grease nipples to lubricate the upper and lower kingpin bearings. Another nipple in the wishbone end lubricates the fulcrum pin bearings at the lower pivot point. A grease nipple was also included in each trackrod end prior to the change of steering rack during 1972. Hubs are fitted with two non-adjustable ball bearing races.

1. Common problems

The front suspension should be near to silent in operation, so any knocks, clunks, creaks or any other strange noises indicate that wear is present. This may be compounded by vibration, steering kick-back, and a less positive feel to the steering and stability. A bias to one side, or a difference in self-centring from full or partial lock may also be due to steering wear or damage. However, this fault may also be caused by the front brakes dragging on one side, tyre problems, or even a misaligned bodyshell. The design of suspension is not very forgiving when worn; you soon know when attention is needed. Follow this check procedure to pinpoint the problem area.

2. Front coil springs

These rarely cause problems, and breakage is very unusual. The springs may settle over an extended period of time resulting in a reduced ride height. During production, the spring free length increased a number of times, so ensure that a correct replacement is used. Some owners fit a spacing washer between

The front spring length was increased as Spridgets put on weight over the years; also to raise the ride height of the Midget 1500. Check that the rubber bump stop cone within the spring is correctly located at the top and is in serviceable condition.

the wishbone and spring location pan to deliberately lower the ride height and improve handling, or even to increase the ride height if one spring has settled. Check for any spacers before buying new springs.

3. Front shock absorber

Check that the three bolts securing the shock absorber body to the mounting platform are tight; these can loosen in service. Do this annually at least. Bounce the front of the car to ensure the shock absorber can control the spring deflection. The movement

Topping up should not be necessary in service, but, if it is, use the correct fluid after checking for leaks. The filler plug must be at the highest point and the lever arm operated slowly to expel air.

The three shock absorber securing bolts should be checked for tightness periodically. Check for fluid leaks and play in the lever arm bearings.

should be arrested within one and a half oscillations. Check for shock absorber fluid leakage around the main spindle bearing where the lever arm is attached. With an assistant to apply the footbrake, pull the car backward and forward a little and observe the lever arm bearing. If the arm has any lateral movement,

Lateral movement in the lever arm indicates worn bearings. Check vertical movement – resistance to change of direction should be felt immediately with no free play.

Hydraulic fluid behind the end cover will indicate leakage past the damper pistons. Time to replace.

the bearing is worn. If these checks reveal a problem, then a new shock absorber will be required. A word of warning here, reconditioned shock absorbers are available but there are quality issues with these. They may not perform well, nor have the service life of a brand new item. Although there is a fluid top up plug, it is not at the highest point of the shock absorber when fitted to the vehicle. Simply topping up in situ will not expel any air present in the system. The unit should never need topping up in service in any case. With a shock absorber disconnected from the upper trunnion, or held in a vice, move the lever arm up and down; there

should be absolutely no free motion when changing direction. If you feel a sudden lack of resistance, then air is present in the fluid space, the internal rocker bearings are worn, or the lever arm is loose on the spindle splines. The end plate of the shock absorber can be removed by taking off six screws; any fluid in the cavity behind the plate will mean the unit is due for replacement.

4. Kingpin and stub axle assembly
The stub axle pivots around the fixed kingpin, via two replaceable liner bushes, each lubricated via external grease nipples. The kingpin and the bushes will wear over time, especially if not lubricated regularly, the lower bush being far more prone to wear.

Disc brake kingpin (1), larger diameter lower bearing, drum brake item (2). Both are worn, showing corrosion attack to lower bearing due to water ingress through the spring-loaded dust excluder tubes. Top trunnion (3) with bearing washer (4) and endfloat shims (5). Original metalastic (6) or polyurethane (yellow here) bushes (7) form the top pivot to the shock absorber lever arm.

The disc brake stub axle incorporates a larger diameter lower bearing than the drum brake stub axle. Also, water can penetrate the lower bearing causing corrosion damage to the kingpin. With the front of the car safely supported clear of the ground, rock the road wheel in the vertical plane. Any wear will be seen and felt, but do not confuse this with play that may be present in the wheel bearing or lower fulcrum pin. Enlist the help of a second pair of eyes to see exactly where the movement is.

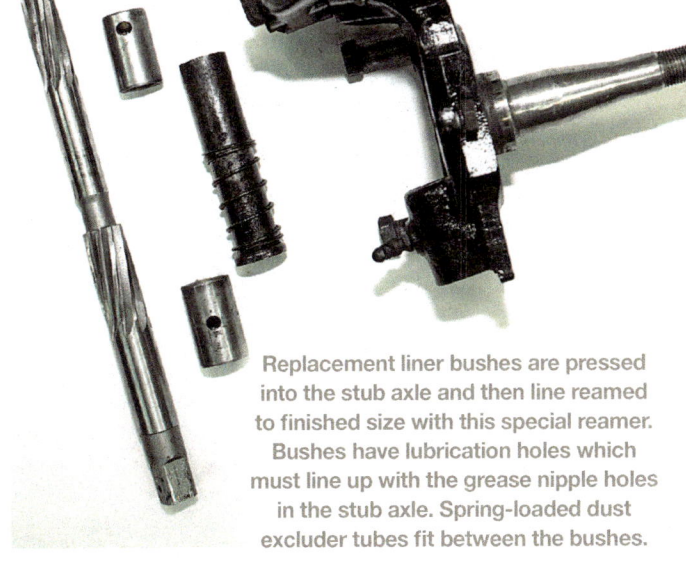

Replacement liner bushes are pressed into the stub axle and then line reamed to finished size with this special reamer. Bushes have lubrication holes which must line up with the grease nipple holes in the stub axle. Spring-loaded dust excluder tubes fit between the bushes.

5. Lower fulcrum pin

This is a threaded pin that rotates within the forked end of the wishbone. The plain centre of the fulcrum pin is secured to the lower end of the kingpin with a tapered cotter pin. Wear will occur on the threaded ends of the fulcrum pin, and the threaded bushes in the wishbone. With the car supported, pull the bottom of the wheel in and out, and look at where the bottom of the kingpin sits within the wishbone. Any movement other than rotational means the pin and bushes are worn. The bushes are a part of the wishbone, and, as such, a complete replacement wishbone will

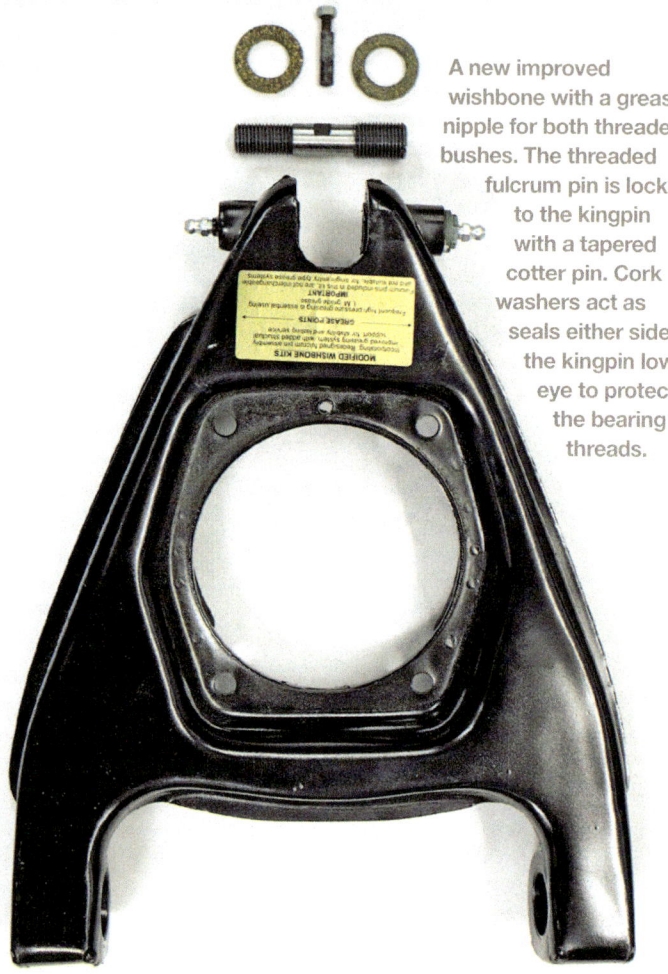

A new improved wishbone with a grease nipple for both threaded bushes. The threaded fulcrum pin is locked to the kingpin with a tapered cotter pin. Cork washers act as seals either side of the kingpin lower eye to protect the bearing threads.

be required, in addition to a new fulcrum pin. Original wishbones were provided with one grease nipple, but now a modified wishbone with a grease nipple for each bush is available. Any wear in the front suspension will require a complete strip down to rectify; it's seldom worth replacing just a single worn component. More often, it's time and cost effective to replace wishbone, fulcrum pin, kingpin, stub axle and trunnion bushes all at once.

6. Top trunnion

This is a solid trunnion mounted to the top of the kingpin, with two metalastic bushes to provide a rotational pivot to the shock absorber lever arm. The bushes can crack and disintegrate over time, allowing unwanted movement in the joint. Polyurethane bushes are available as a modification to improve handling, but may increase noise and vibration transmitted to the vehicle. The top trunnion requires shims to be added to correctly set the vertical endfloat of the stub axle. Too much shimming will result in excessive endfloat, whilst too little may result in the stub axle binding against the top trunnion bearing washer. If the steering requires excessive force and is slow to self-centre, then check the freedom of movement for each stub axle in relation to the top trunnion. A modified version of the trunnion is available which increases the angle of negative camber. Primarily intended for motorsport usage, when this is used on public roads, increased bump steer or 'tramlining' may be experienced, along with increased tyre wear. Also, the self-centring action of the steering may be affected.

7. Front anti-roll bar

When fitted, this is usually a reliable item, but wear in the drop link and frame mounting rubber bushes can occur. Pulling on the bar and links will reveal such wear. The mounting brackets

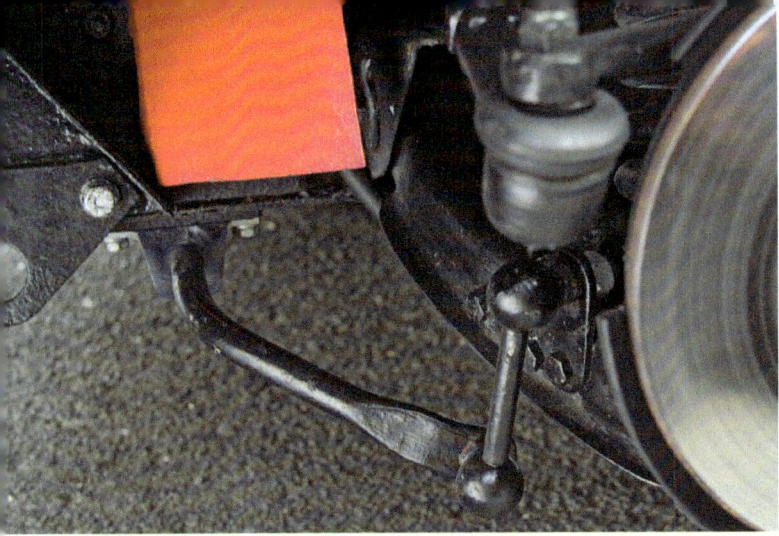

to the front frame rails can be damaged by impacts, so check here for distortion or pulled mounting screws. Note that larger diameter anti-roll bars may be fitted as a modification to increase roll stiffness. Use the correct rubber bushes for the diameter of bar fitted. Polyurethane bushes are available as a modification to further improve the effectiveness of the anti-roll bar.

8. Front wheel bearings

This check is similar to that of the kingpin, but now you're looking for movement between the wheel and the stub axle assembly. Spin the hub to check for any roughness or noise. The wheel bearings are non-adjustable ball races, so any wear will necessitate replacement. Wheel bearings can generate a low rumbling noise when worn. Check also for leakage of grease from the hub seal.

9. Steering

The rack and pinion unit fitted until January 1972 is a very reliable unit and as long as the rubber gaiters are in good order there is little to worry about. The lubrication nipple fitted to one side of the rack is for 80 grade oil, not grease. Although the trackrod ends are provided with grease nipples, these can wear over time, causing steering play, tyre wear and clunking noises. Have an assistant waggle the steering wheel whilst you watch for any movement in the joint. Any play will be felt in the steering wheel. The later type steering rack, post-January 1972, is more likely to suffer internal wear than the earlier type (the trackrod ends were now sealed for life without any grease nipples). Place a hand on the trackrod as your assistant waggles the steering wheel; you may feel wear within the inner ball joints inside the gaiters. Check the condition of the trackrod end rubber gaiters as well as the main rack gaiters regularly.

The anti-roll bar drop link bushes have rubber ball end inserts. If worn or perished, the drop link must be replaced.

The anti-roll bar bracket can easily suffer impact damage if grounded. Inspect rubber bushes as well.

Regular greasing is essential to drive out moisture and prevent wear. Use a good quality high pressure grease gun.

loadings, such as occur when removing the steering wheel with the aid of a hammer. If there is longitudinal movement of the steering wheel, the column has probably been damaged and should be replaced.

Check also for any vertical movement of the steering wheel, indicating that the upper column bearing is worn. Finally, check the clamp bolt at the base of the column where it connects with the rack input splined shaft; any lost motion in the steering wheel may be due to a loose clamp bolt.

11. Steering alignment

Ordinarily, only the tracking angle is checked and adjusted. Modern, four-wheel laser alignment measuring equipment is highly accurate, but is not in itself a full geometric check. This does not check camber or castor angles, ride height errors or static wheel loadings. Steering that fails to provide feel or respond correctly may require a more comprehensive measurement check from a specialist. Certainly, cars being set up for race circuit use should be fully checked in this way.

10. Steering column

For the North American market, the original single piece steering column shaft was changed to a collapsible, energy-absorbing item in January 1968. This was required to meet new safety regulations. UK market Spridgets continued to use the single-piece column until the introduction of the round rear wheelarch Midget from GAN5-105501. This was now a two-piece collapsible column, but without the energy-absorbing section of the export column. Both the energy-absorbing and plain collapsible columns must not be subjected to shock end

12. Exchange components

Although stripping and rebuilding the front suspension and steering unit is fairly straightforward, reconditioning individual components is a specialised task. Reconditioned items in exchange for worn ones may provide a much cheaper option than buying new. Common items available as exchange units are shock absorbers, steering rack and pinion, wishbones, and re-bushed stub axles. However, the serviceable life of reconditioned items is not necessarily be the same as new and original items.

Models prior to the introduction of HAN8/GAN3, in March 1964, used a quarter-elliptic rear spring with an upper radius arm to locate the top of the rear axle. A lever arm shock absorber is connected to the axle via a rubber bushed link. From March 1964, a more conventional semi-elliptic spring was fitted but without the upper radius arm.

1. Quarter-elliptic suspension problems

An unequal ride height from side to side is a common feature with this pre-1964 system. The short length of the spring leaves means a high loading force. This often results in rapid spring settlement and eventual leaf breakage. The driver's side of the car is more vulnerable to this due to the weight of the driver always being aboard. The manufacturer did produce a special wedge piece to place under the spring and balance an unequal ride height – rather cheaper than replacing the spring should the owner complain. The early-type spring was made up of 15 leaves; this was superseded by an 11 leaf spring with much thicker leaves that seemed to cure the problem of excessive settlement and breakage. It is not unusual for the springs to creak in usage, regular cleaning and lubricating of the leaves is a good idea. This attention will also provide a regular check for any breakages. However, anything more than a creaking sound needs to be investigated just in case a leaf has broken. An unequal ride height can also be

Check the quarter-elliptic rear spring for signs of sagging and cracked leaves. Check also the lever arm shock absorber, just inboard of the spring, for signs of leakage. The two securing bolts should also be checked for tightness.

The spring anchor plate should be parallel to the lower edge of the sill when viewed side-on. If it's not, corrosion has weakened the surrounding structure, with the result that the spring location box has moved and lowered ride height. The anchor plate must be re-set to the correct position before welding in new metal.

caused by the spring location box moving within the rear bulkhead. This is due to serious corrosion weakening the surrounding metalwork in this highly stressed region. This is a serious structural problem and will require extensive repair work properly carried out. The bottom of the spring

The semi-elliptic spring should also be inspected for sagging and broken leaves. Check the tightness of the axle U-bolts. These do loosen following replacement, upsetting the steering. Again, any rusting around the attachment points requires an immediate and proper repair.

mounting plate should be parallel to the lower edge of the sill; if not, the location box will have moved. The radius arm bushes can wear out, causing noise from excessive axle movement as the location becomes sloppy. The hollow section radius arms can rust through from the inside and eventually break, leaving the axle unsupported laterally. You will certainly notice this from the driving seat. If the rear axle takes over steering the car, check the radius arms. Also check the tightness of the rear spring 'U' clamp nuts, and the bolts passing through the spring to the top clamp.

2. Semi-elliptic suspension problems

The 1964 change to this type of rear spring provided a better ride quality and lateral spring location. The handling became less tail-sensitive. The semi-elliptic spring proved more reliable and quieter

in service, although still prone to settlement and leaf breakage over a greater period of time. Any noise or peculiar steering effect can indicate a spring leaf failure. The rear of the spring is located by a swing shackle fitted with rubber bushes. This rarely gives any trouble although it is wise to replace the bushes when changing a spring. Following a spring change, the axle U-bolts should be re-checked for tightness, as they do loosen after a short while. Any feeling of rear end steering may be caused by this.

3. Rear shock absorbers

These seldom give any trouble, but as with the front units, check for fluid leakage where the lever arm and spindle meet. Check the rubber-bushed drop link, as perishing of the rubber bushes will produce some clonking noises. A popular modification is to replace the lever arm shock absorbers with telescopic shock absorbers. A conversion kit is available, but do ensure that when

fitted, the exhaust pipe has sufficient clearance in relation to full axle movement. Check the tightness of the all the securing bolts.

4. Bump stop and check straps

The axle is cushioned on compression by a rubber bump stop located above the axle. Ensure that the rubber is in good condition and secure. The check strap prevents the axle from dropping when the car is jacked up or flying over a humpback bridge. Again, check its condition and security.

5. Modified axle locations

In addition, a Panhard rod to control lateral movement of the axle can be fitted. This is a transverse link with one end pivoted to the floor and the other to the axle. However, not all owners agree that this is worth fitting for normal road use. A Panhard rod must be fitted properly and securely. Similarly, a Watts linkage will serve the same purpose but retain a better geometry of the axle; requiring two attachment points to the floor and a central attachment to the axle. Anti-tramp bars can also be fitted to semi-elliptic sprung versions, but mounted below the spring. These can be vulnerable to grounding on uneven surfaces. Seek proper advice before attempting to modify the rear suspension – some modifications are not entirely suitable for normal road usage and require specialist fitting.

Check the bump stop rubber (1) and the check strap (2). The radius arm (3) for the quarter-elliptic versions should also be checked for corrosion. If the metalastic bushes at each end wear out, the rear axle may take over steering the car. You will hear plenty of awful noise too.

Be aware that anti-tramp bars reduce ground clearance. Note the uprated halfshaft fitted to this axle, and the telescopic shock absorber.

When accelerating hard, especially on uneven surfaces, an anti-tramp bar fitted below the rear semi-elliptic spring will maintain the axle location. Note the lower location for the replacement telescopic shock-absorber.

The fabricated steel axle casing is fitted with a differential gear set, mounted in a cast aluminium housing. This can be removed from the axle casing with the axle still in place in the car. Steel halfshafts transmit power to the rear wheels, mounted on single ball race bearing hubs. The hubs are secured to the axle by a large central nut, the left-hand side having a left-hand thread. The hubs also carry the oil seal and wheel mounting studs. Three sets of final drive ratio were used during production:

4.22:1	From AN5-501 onwards	May 1958
3.9:1	From HAN9-77591 and GAN4-66226	December 1968
3.7:1	From GAN6-200001	August 1977

These are interchangeable within axle casings. Other ratios were available from the manufacturer for competition use, including a limited-slip differential set. The ratio can be established from the numbers stamped into the housing above the brake pipe 'T' piece mounting hole. This gives the number of gear teeth on the crownwheel and pinion.

The wire wheel option required a narrower rear axle casing to be fitted with different halfshafts and hub assemblies. The axle casing required different location brackets with the change from quarter-elliptic to semi-elliptic springs; these are not interchangeable. With a change to the handbrake operating linkage introduced in August 1976, a total of six variants of axle casing were used.

The number of gear teeth on the pinion and crownwheel is stamped on both the aluminium casing and crownwheel. A simple calculation will give you the final drive ratio. The casing is stamped just above the brake pipe union securing hole.

1. Common problems – oil leaks

Oil leakage from the rear hub seals can go unnoticed until the oil contaminates the rear brake linings, causing a loss of rear brake performance. The brakes may produce a warning squeal as the linings become contaminated. Regular checks of the rear brakes, by removing the brake drums, is therefore important. The axle is fitted with a vent on the top of the casing on the right-hand tube.

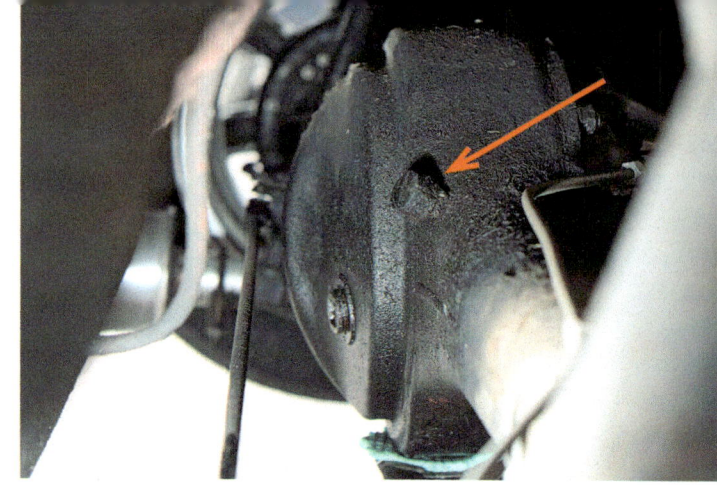

The axle breather is situated on the right-hand side of the differential, part way along the halfshaft tube. Remove the cap and check that the breather is not blocked.

Check that this is not blocked, causing the axle to pressurise as it warms up. The input shaft oil seal can also leak, but replacing this may upset the input shaft bearing preload setting. Consult the workshop manual before attempting this job.

2. Final drive noise

It is not unusual to experience a small amount of gear whine from the rear axle, but this should only be very slight. It is a specialised job to correctly adjust the mesh of the crownwheel and pinion set, in order to obtain silent running. If noise is excessive, you need to replace the differential assembly. The wheel bearings can produce a dull rumble when worn, but are fairly easy to change. Ensure that new oil seals are fitted the correct way around in the hubs when renewing.

3. Halfshafts

Early-type halfshafts were prone to breakage, even with the 42.5bhp of the 948cc engine. Nowadays, most of these early shafts have been replaced by a later, stronger type. The later type shaft can be identified by the part number BTA 806 cast into the end (visible within the central hole of the brake drum for steel wheel versions). The shaft usually breaks at the inner

The pinion oil seal can leak, but replacing it may upset the setting of the input shaft bearings. The universal joints can wear, but are fairly easy to renew. Getting the shaft back into the pre-Midget 1500 versions is the really tricky bit!

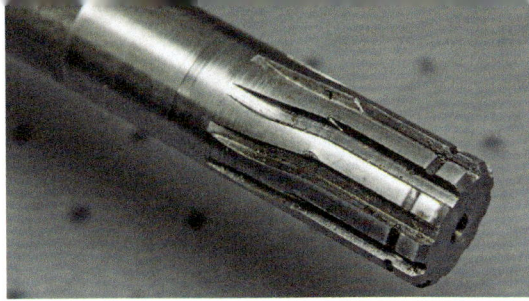

Caught just in time. The inner end of this halfshaft is twisted. Left much longer, it would have sheared off. The differential would then have to be removed to recover the broken end.

An uprated halfshaft with a shrunk-on tapered flange with securing nut. This is a direct replacement, able to handle a lot more torque than an original shaft.

end, so that the differential unit must be removed to recover the broken end. Wire wheel halfshafts seem to be stronger but breakage is not unknown. There are special shafts available today to cope with very high power outputs for Spridgets which have been fitted with modern twin-cam engines.

4. Wire wheel halfshafts

These differ from the steel wheel halfshafts in having a spline at each end, the outer end being a press fit into the splined hub. The hub splines can wear within the wheel, causing a clicking noise when accelerating or braking. Less commonly, the shaft to hub spline can occasionally become a loose fit and emit additional

The wire wheel halfshaft and hub. Check the wheel location splines for wear. The left-hand shaft has a right-hand thread securing the wheel, and the right-hand side a left-hand thread. Ensure that the correct hub/shaft combination is fitted on each side. Check also that the hub is tight to the halfshaft splined ends.

clicking and clunking noises. This may require the replacement of both hub and shaft.

5. Propeller shaft

The front portion of the propshaft runs within an enclosed tunnel, making the front universal joint (UJ) inaccessible on pre-Midget 1500 models. Wear in the front or rear UJ can cause vibration in the propshaft; felt by the driver in a similar way to tyre imbalance. If badly worn, a sharp clunking noise will be heard on the transition from acceleration to overrun, when changing gear and when pulling away from rest. The Midget 1500 has a bolted flange coupling from the gearbox to the front UJ. An access hole is provided in the floor beneath the front UJ to allow the flange to be unbolted. Earlier versions have a splined shaft connection to the gearbox; the shaft can simply be pulled out once the rear UJ is released from the differential input shaft. Getting it back in is a different matter – no hole is provided to allow access to guide the front of the shaft into the gearbox. Some owners resort to cutting a hole in the tunnel to gain access. However, the shaft can be re-inserted without having to cut any holes or to remove the engine and gearbox. Using a homemade tool, the front UJ can be gripped and the shaft guided into the gearbox rear bearing. Once engaged, the tool can

then be pulled away from the UJ. Early models had a grease nipple fitted to each universal joint; this was replaced by sealed for life joints from June 1965. All replacement universal joints are of the sealed for life type and are fairly easy and inexpensive to change.

Early versions had universal joints that could be greased. An access hole is provided for this purpose.

A homemade tool that simply clips around the front UJ yoke to guide the propshaft into the gearbox rear bearing. Once installed, the tool is pulled away.

The Lockheed, four-wheel hydraulically-operated braking system is supplemented by a mechanical parking brake operating on the rear wheels. Four-wheel drum-type brakes were used until the introduction of the HAN7/GAN2 (October 1962) versions when disc-type front brakes were adopted. The hydraulic system was single-circuit on UK versions until May 1978 when a twin-circuit system was introduced. North American versions used a twin-circuit system from November 1967. This system was divided into individual front and rear circuits. A brake servo was never fitted by the factory; however, some owners have subsequently fitted a vacuum servo to reduce the force required on the brake pedal.

1. Brake fluid

Traditionally, a mineral-based brake fluid was used. However, some owners now prefer to use a silicon-based fluid, which is impervious to moisture absorption, and therefore a better protection against internal corrosion of the hydraulic system. The two types are totally incompatible and must not be mixed. Silicon fluid should only be used following a complete replacement of all the hydraulic components. Make sure you know which type is in the system before doing any maintenance work. Mineral oil should be changed periodically according to the manufacturer's instructions – usually around every three years.

Be very careful not to spill mineral brake fluid; it is a good paint remover. Hiding beside the heater blower fan, the early-type master cylinder can be awkward to top up from most fluid containers.

2. Hydraulic fluid leakage

The fluid in the master cylinder should be checked regularly, and any noticeable or rapid loss of fluid level should be investigated immediately. However, the level will drop very gradually as the front disc brake pads wear. Leaks can occur from the wheel cylinders within the brake drums. A loss of braking performance may be noticed as leaking fluid contaminates the friction linings on the brake shoes. Steering pulling to one side or a squeaking sound on brake application are signs that need to be heeded. If the brake pedal develops a spongy feel, it is an indication of air in the hydraulic system or water contaminated fluid. A leaking master cylinder can be checked by pulling back the dust seal where the operating rod enters the cylinder. Should you see any fluid leakage, or an oily patch on the floor beneath the brake pedal, then the master cylinder will require immediate attention. On the separate brake and clutch master cylinder versions, the pedal box cover plate will need to be removed to check for leakage – it's a good idea to do this as a part of each service.

The operating length of the pushrods and pedal return height are set by the adjusting screws on initial build. These should not be re-set in an attempt to overcome other problems within the braking and clutch systems. Check for fluid leakage where the pushrods enter the cylinder, and that the return springs are effective.

3. Combined master cylinder problems

The combined brake and clutch master cylinder is provided with adjustment of the operating pushrods. The correct adjustment is set on initial fitting and should not be adjusted in service in an attempt to overcome other problems. Both pushrods must have a small amount of free play to allow both hydraulic pistons to fully return to the end of the cylinders. If this free play is eliminated, the pistons may not return fully, allowing fluid to be trapped in the system, thereby causing brake or clutch drag as the system remains partially pressurised. Excessive free play of the pushrods causes increased pedal travel, and the clutch may not disengage fully. Check for wear in the pedal clevis pin holes and the clevis pins. The pedals swivel on a common pivot bolt which can also wear; check for sideways movement of the pedals. Conversely, with a lack of use, the pedals may seize to the pivot bolt. Depressing one pedal may cause the other pedal to move or the pivot bolt to rotate in the pedal box. Check for free and independent movement of the pedals, and security of the pivot bolt in the pedal box. If the vehicle is used with the pedals

Check that both brake and clutch pedals move freely from one another, and that the pivot bolt is tight. Also, check for sideways movement indicating that the pedal bushes and pivot bolt are worn. Any signs of brake fluid dripping here mean that the master cylinder seals need replacing.

and pivot bolt seized or partially seized, vehicle safety will be compromised and the pedal box may become damaged. Ensure that the pedal return springs are fitted between each pushrod and the front of the pedal box. It must be stressed that two types of combined master cylinder are used – the earlier drum brake version has a ⅞in bore and the disc brake version having a ¾in bore. It is essential to match the correct cylinder to the type of wheel brake employed. It is also important to note that the operating pushrods are of different lengths for both types.

4. Single master cylinder problems

The original single-circuit type master cylinder contained a steel cylindrical fluid reservoir. Replacement cylinders now have a plastic reservoir; this reduces corrosion contamination of the fluid and provides a visual check of fluid level. The top cover of the pedal box assembly must be removed to check for any leakage around the pushrod seal and wear of the clevis pin at the top of

With the cover plate removed, check for leakage from around the pushrods. The fluid level in the reservoir will drop as the brake pads wear, but only very gradually. Don't be tempted to top-up – the reservoir will overflow when new pads are fitted.

the pedal. As with the combined type master cylinder, check that both clutch and brake pedals move freely and independently of each other, and that the pivot pin bolt is secure and not allowing sideways movement of the pedals. The pedal return springs are fitted under the top footwell panel; ensure they are properly attached.

5. Hydraulic cylinder mismatch

All hydraulic systems are carefully designed to ensure that the piston diameters of master and slave cylinders are in correct ratio and appropriate for the application. To alter the relationship between any of the piston diameters will upset both the pressure ratio and amount of travel of the operating levers. Hence, changing any of the vehicle hydraulic cylinders from the designed size, will affect the amount of pedal travel and pressure applied to the pedal, as well as to the friction linings in the brakes. It is therefore important to ensure only the correct hydraulic components are fitted for each model. The effectiveness, safety and the feel of the braking system may otherwise be compromised.

It is common for owners of early drum brake models to convert to the later disc front brakes. To do this correctly, the master cylinder and rear wheel cylinders must also be changed for the disc brake compatible type. Externally, brake cylinders can be difficult to identify in relation to piston diameter. Any modifications to the hydraulic system must be correctly applied. A system which appears to be in good condition on inspection, but fails to operate satisfactorily, may well have an incorrect component fitted. Seek advice from an owners' club or specialist if you suspect modifications have been made incorrectly, or if you intend to make any modifications to the braking system.

6. Worn friction linings

A loss of braking performance and a shrill squeak are signs that the lining material may have worn dangerously thin. Also, this could be due to contamination from leaking rear axle oil, front hub grease or brake fluid. Regular servicing inspections should therefore be made to monitor the condition of the lining material. Check that drum brake lining securing rivets are not loose or coming into contact with the drum. Brake friction lining dust will build-up within the brake drum if not cleaned out periodically. This too can affect braking performance and create noise. Check the brake drum and brake disc surface for scoring and corrosion. When renewing any of the friction linings, check the brake pedal travel before driving. It may take several pumps of the brake pedal to bring new front brake pads into contact with the disc when the calliper pistons have been fully retracted. When retracting calliper pistons, check that the master cylinder does not spill brake fluid. Always work on one side at a time, and pump the pedal before starting on the opposite brake to prevent the possibility of fluid spillage.

7. Pulling to one side

Both cylinder mismatch and worn friction linings can cause this. In addition, poorly adjusted drum brakes, or seized or sticking slave cylinder pistons or disc brake pistons may be to blame. Brake pads can stick in the calliper. A constriction in a flexible brake hose is less common, but not unknown. Furthermore, worn steering components, imbalanced tyre pressures, mismatched tyres, tyre condition and, more seriously, a misaligned bodyshell can all be suspects.

8. Vibration when braking

A badly worn or corroded brake drum or brake disc can cause such vibration. This may also be felt through the brake pedal as a

Check the brake disc for wear, corrosion and run-out. Use a dial indicator for the latter. Check also the condition of the brake pads and the flexible hose for perishing and tyre rubbing. Here, a stainless steel braided hose is fitted, which is claimed to last longer, and provide a more positive feel to the pedal.

rhythmic pulsing action. The front brake discs should be checked for any run-out with a dial indicator gauge; this should not be more than around 0.008in. Rear brake drums can become oval if the handbrake is heavily applied when the drums are very hot. It is unwise to leave the vehicle stored for long periods with the handbrake on: chock the wheels instead. It should be noted, too, that some replacement brake drums have been found to have an oversize location diameter. These may not centralise properly to the hub location diameter, the lack of concentricity resulting in vibration. The drum should be a snug fit to the hub.

9. Excessive brake pedal travel

This may be caused by the drum brakes requiring adjustment. There is no automatic adjustment on the Lockheed system fitted. Manual adjustment is provided by snail cam adjusters accessed via rubber plugs in each brake drum. The adjuster cam peaks

Front drum brake adjusters are accessible through a hole in both wheel and brake drum (clockwise to tighten). Do not actually adjust with the drum removed. With the drum removed, clean out brake dust and check the cylinders for signs of leakage.

The snail cam adjuster for front drum and earlier rear drum brakes. The cam peaks and locating ridge can wear sufficiently for the adjuster to slip back.

the pedal. With the earlier combined brake and clutch master cylinder, incorrect adjustment of the pushrod may allow excessive pedal travel. Disc brakes are self-adjusting. If the pedal is both low and has a spongy feel, then check for a fluid leak in the system.

10. Brakes sticking on

This can be cause by sticking or seized wheel cylinders or disc brake calliper pistons. Also, the flexible hoses can suffer interior deterioration to the extent that they act as non-return valves. The hoses will allow high pressure fluid to pass to the wheel cylinder, but may restrict the return flow when the brake pedal is released. As described previously, the adjustment of the master cylinder pushrod must allow the piston to return fully to the end

can wear away, and allow the brake adjustment to slip back a notch or more. The cam peaks should be inspected to ensure that the profile is still serviceable. From HAN6-20792 and GAN1-13555 (May 1962) the rear brakes were changed from a single- to twin-piston slave cylinder. The snail cam adjuster was replaced by a cone and expanding tappet adjuster, with a square-headed screw on the inward face of the brake backplate. The adjuster screw can seize if neglected, and the square head can be easily damaged if the correct type of adjusting tool is not used. The screw thread of the adjuster should be lubricated with copper grease, and operated occasionally to prevent seizure. The pivot pins and holes in the brake pedal can also wear, allowing increased movement of

The handbrake expanding link fits between the brake shoes; the pivot (indicated by screwdiver) can easily seize, rendering the handbrake ineffective. This may also cause the handbrake to stick on if the car has been left inactive for an extended period.

of the cylinder to clear the internal drilling from the reservoir.

Ensure that adjustment of drum brakes does not result in any binding when the brake pedal is released. Check that all brake shoe return springs are correctly fitted. Make sure the handbrake is fully released and again, that any adjustment to the handbrake mechanism allows the rear drums to rotate freely when the lever is released. A car that has been left inactive is more likely to suffer from corrosion forming on the friction surfaces. If slight, this will free up with a little gentle usage, but if sticking persists, along with any imbalance, vibration or noise, investigate immediately. Inactivity may result in the handbrake pivots seizing, as well as the brake pedal pivot bolt in the pedal box.

11. Excessive handbrake travel & ineffective service

Rear brake shoe adjustment should be checked first. Then inspect the condition of the lining material for wear and contamination. Check the brake drum rubbing surface for scoring, corrosion and dust build-up. The early single piston slave cylinder should be free to slide in the backplate, allowing centralisation of the shoes. If this is seized, remove the cylinder retaining clips, and free off the sliding faces. Lightly lubricate with copper grease on reassembly. The later twin-piston slave cylinder has an expanding link between the shoes for handbrake application. The pivot in this link can seize and render the handbrake inoperative. It can seize in either the off or on positions, hence it is good practice not to leave the handbrake on during long periods of storage.

The handbrake compensator on the rear axle can develop wear in the thread between bracket and vertical swivel pillar. This, combined with wear in the operating rod clevis pins and eyes, can produce excessive handbrake lever movement. A small amount of adjustment is provided at the bracket end of the cable, but always eliminate any wear before adjusting.

Remove the left-hand seat to inspect the handbrake mounting bracket for security and any cracking. The two countersunk screws holding the lever mounting often loosen.

Trying to remove a brake drum with the brake linings expanded is not an easy job. Remove the two-piece link to free off the pivot and, again, lightly lubricate. Next, check all the handbrake mechanism clevis pins and rod holes for wear. Accumulative wear in all of the pivot points can have quite an effect on handbrake lever travel. The compensator on the rear axle can also wear, so observe this whilst an assistant operates the handbrake. The problem of accumulative wear in the handbrake linkage was addressed from August 1976 when the compensator and linkage was replaced by a revised cable arrangement. The handbrake cable does have provision for some adjustment, but this is really only for the initial setting-up. If the handbrake linkage is worn, then this should be attended to rather than adjusting the cable. Check the bracket that secures the lever to the transmission tunnel. This can loosen and crack. Check the security of the three screws holding the bracket and the two screws holding the lever to the bracket. The seat must be removed to gain access.

12. Knocking sound from the rear brakes

The single-piston slave cylinder was replaced by a twin-piston cylinder from HAN6-20792 and GAN1-13555 (May 1962). This was held to the brake backplate with a 'C' shaped spring clip. This clip can loosen, allowing the slave

The later type rear drum brake slave cylinders are retained by this C-clip. These often loosen, allowing the cylinder to move sufficiently to contact the rotating hub. These clips are notoriously difficult to fit properly: three tangs must engage in the groove.

cylinder to move sufficiently to contact the rotating hub, causing a rhythmic knocking sound. This type of clip can be very awkward to fit properly, and may become strained and weakened when the cylinder is replaced.

13. Brake light operation

The single-circuit brake system utilised a pressure switch in the main distribution union. This completes the circuit to the brake lights when the system is pressurised by the brake pedal. The switch can fail, but this can be easily checked. With the ignition switched on, connect both the cables at the switch together. If the lights operate, then the switch is faulty and must be replaced. As the switch screws directly into the hydraulic circuit, the system will need to be bled before use. Some remanufactured switches seem to have a reduced life so check the operation of the brake lights regularly. North American twin-circuit systems and UK Midget 1500 versions used a mechanically-operated brake light switch mounted in the pedal box and operated from the brake pedal. With a bit of work, this type of switch can be used on the single-circuit versions. In addition to improved reliability, the brake lights will operate as soon as the pedal is moved, rather than at a pre-determined line pressure in the system, which can increase as the switch ages.

The hydraulic brake light switch can fail, some replacement items have been found to be very short lived. The brake circuit must be bled after replacing the switch.

The Midget 1500 and post-1968 North American versions have a pedal-operated brake light switch, mounted in the front of the pedal box. A good modification to make to earlier versions with a pressure-operated switch. The box will have to be removed to drill the mounting hole.

14. Twin-circuit failure warning

The North American twin-circuit brake system is fitted with a front to rear pressure differential switch to warn of a failure in one of the circuits. If one circuit fails to pressurise fully, the switch causes the dashboard warning light to illuminate. An immediate investigation of the hydraulic system will then be required.

15. Pipework

From new, steel Bundy pipework and flexible reinforced rubber hoses were fitted. The Bundy pipes tend to corrode, eventually requiring replacement. Many owners replace with copper pipework which resists corrosion. Check that any new pipework is properly fitted, secured, and clear of any moving parts of the steering and suspension. Watch out for any kinks where a sharp radius has been poorly formed. The flexible hoses can suffer external cracking and internal restriction after prolonged use. Many owners now fit stainless steel braided hoses which have a much smaller external diameter, and are claimed to improve the feel of the brake pedal. Watch out for any chafing of flexible hoses when turning the front wheels through full right- and left-hand lock.

Back view of the front drum brake. Check the interconnecting hydraulic pipe (1) for corrosion and the flexible hose (2) for perishing and tyre rub. Brakes sticking on for no apparent reason may be due to the internal condition of the flexible hose. If in doubt, always replace; inexpensive and easy.

All versions use a 13in dia road wheel, but of varying width and pattern. The AN5, HAN6, GAN1 and very early HAN7 and GAN2 versions used a 3.5in wide wheel with 12 ventilation holes. From December 1962, this was replaced by a plain steel wheel of the same width. With the introduction of the Facelift versions in October 1969 (HAN10/GAN5), a 4.5in wide wheel of Rostyle pattern became the standard fitment. This was replaced by a second generation of Rostyle wheel with the introduction of the round rear wheelarch Midget. The latter remained the standard wheel for the remainder of production. A 4in wide, 60-spoke wire wheel became available as an option shortly after the introduction of the HAN7/GAN2 versions. This necessitated the use of special splined hubs and a narrower rear axle casing. Standard tyre sizes were 5.20 x 13in crossply, to be replaced by 145 x 13in radial ply tyres from the late 1960s.

1. Steel wheel problems

Vibration through the steering wheel at speed is usually associated with tyre imbalance, but this is not the only cause. A buckled wheel rim or a wheel running out of true can also cause

All steel-wheeled Midgets wore plain chromed hub caps until Rostyle wheels were introduced in 1969.

The first generation Rostyle wheel introduced in October 1969 increased wheel width to 4.5in The centre caps can loosen, causing a faint tinkling sound at low speed.

The second generation Rostyle (Rubery Owen style) wheel from 1972 to end of production. Other than rim damage and rust formation through the paint, check the condition of the metal around the wheel nut area.

steering vibration. Check both the inside and the outside of each rim, and spin each wheel to check for run-out. Vibration can also be caused by worn universal joints in the prop-shaft. The early-type steel wheels can suffer from cracking around the securing stud holes, so look very carefully for this. All types of steel wheel will eventually lose paint and become rusty, but they can be shot-blasted and repainted. Rostyles, due to the intricacies of the application of the black and silver finish, require rather more work to refurbish. A light tinkling sound heard at low speed may be the Rostyle wheel centre caps becoming loose.

2. Wire wheel problems

Wire wheels look great when new but eventually develop problems with loosening spokes and wearing of the locating splines in the hub. A clicking sound from the wheel when accelerating or braking

Wire wheels really look the part but can develop numerous problems in later life. Early versions had 'eared spinners' but safety concerns saw the introduction of octagonal nuts. Exactly how many pedestrians have suffered flailed legs from early wire-wheeled Spridgets is unrecorded!

is an indication that the hub splines are worn. Both a new wheel centre and hub may be required, which will be expensive. This type of wheel is difficult to keep clean and rust can soon take hold. Wire wheels also require an inner tube to be fitted because the spokes prevent an airtight seal. Balancing wire wheels may prove difficult if spoke tension and rim run-out are not correct. Wire wheels originally had a silver/aluminium painted finish, but around 1970, North America versions had chrome-plated wire wheels for a short time. Initially, the wheels were secured with two-eared, or winged, spinners. A copper faced mallet was supplied to turn these. However, safety concerns lead to the universal change to octagonal securing nuts that required a special spanner and a mallet to be used. The right-hand wheels are secured by left-hand threads, and the direction of tightening and loosening are shown on the spinner or nut.

This Midget 1500 has chromed wire wheels that fit directly to the original wheel studs without an adaptor hub. Note the four wheel nuts, and absence of either an eared spinner or octagonal nut for location.

3. Aftermarket wire wheels

For owners wishing to have the traditional look of wire wheels without needing to change the rear axle and brake discs, a bolt-on adaptor kit was introduced by the support industry. Here, a steel wheel version could have special splined adaptors bolted on directly to the existing hub assemblies. Some of these have been around for a number of years now and may be in need of attention. This could cause some confusion when ordering replacement parts, as they are not the same as the manufacturer's original pattern. A simplified option is wire wheels that are located by the original wheel studs, dispensing with the need for a splined hub altogether.

3. Alloy wheels

Not fitted originally, but now a very popular modification to replace rusty steel wheels or the expensive to restore wire wheels. They are available in wider rim widths than the original wheels, but may create a clearance problem on square rear

Modern alloy wheels are a popular replacement for wobbly wires or rusty Rostyles, the traditional 'Minilite' look being very common. Whatever the type or style, ensure the correct wheel nuts are used.

wheelarch versions, particularly if the rear suspension is lower than standard. Some wire wheels require special wheel nuts or spacers to be fitted, depending on the amount of rim offset.

Alloy wheels can bring problems of their own, however. Being made from a soft alloy, the rims can be very easily damaged by kerbing. Some alloys are quite susceptible to corrosion, too, and must be kept clean and free of brake dust. Corrosion can form where the tyre bead seals against the rim; this can become serious enough to allow a loss of air pressure from the tyre.

4. Wheel stud problems

The standard wheel stud has a ⅜in UNF thread and is quite easily stripped if over-tightened, or removed extensively. Fitting new studs is fairly easy, but it is vital to check wheel nut tightness shortly after new studs have been fitted. These do ease off and a clicking from the wheels is a sure sign that the wheel nuts have become loose. Check regularly until you are satisfied that tightness is being maintained. The nuts should also be replaced at the same time as fitting new studs. Take note that the seating face profile of the wheel nuts will vary, some being conical and others rounded. Only use the correct nut for the type of wheel fitted.

5. Tyre problems

Just the usual observations with tyres concerning pressure, wear, side wall cracking and carcass damage. Front tyres wearing on the inner or outer edges are a sign of incorrect tracking alignment, and require the steering to be investigated for wear and realignment. An out of balance tyre will manifest itself with vibration through the steering, but do ensure that the problem is not a wire wheel that has developed a spoke tension problem.

With the growing popularity of alloy wheels, many owners are fitting much wider tyres than the car was designed to run with. You can overdo this; the standard suspension is not designed to cope with high grip tyres and may cause a sudden loss of control, if the suspension deflects under a much higher force being applied. At the limit, and not on the public road of course, Spridgets are more at home sliding around corners with controlled degrees of understeer or oversteer, rather than being 'on rails' and then jumping off the track unexpectedly. Any drastic changes in the type of tyre will require the suspension to be properly modified to cope. If the car has been left standing for a long period of time, the tyres can develop a flat spot, particularly if full air pressure is not maintained.

All versions used a 12-volt electrical system as supplied by Lucas. A positive earth (ground) return was used until November 1967, a negative earth return thereafter. For the UK market, an alternator replaced the dynamo from December 1972. Some overseas markets were equipped with an alternator prior to this. Dynamo equipped cars required a voltage control unit between the battery and dynamo. Early versions used a two-sbobbin control unit, a three-bobbin unit being introduced in October 1969. Main circuits were protected by two fuses, increased to four from October 1969. The system was typical of the industry standard of the time and thanks to the simplicity of the electrical equipment, generally only suffers fairly basic, age-related problems. Perhaps the biggest problem is the addition of improperly fitted electrical equipment.

1. Common problems – battery

The battery is the heart of the system and, unless it maintains its capacity, can cause problems in starting. The battery voltage can be checked with a multimeter: a healthy battery should provide around 13V. However, this is only a partial check, the true state of the battery is determined by the rate of voltage drop off when under load and subsequent recovery. A hydrometer can be used to measure the specific gravity of the electrolyte in each cell (not sealed for life batteries). This should be around 1280 – any less indicates a low state of charge in one or more cells. Essentially, a battery over three years old could be past its best. When the starter motor shows signs of labouring, a new battery may be required.

Period-style batteries like this are filled with sulphuric acid and expel hydrogen gas when being charged: they must be treated with caution. Battery access is much improved without the optional heater.

It is essential that the battery terminal posts are kept free of corrosive deposits, which would reduce conductivity and impede the flow of the high current required to operate the starter.

2. Jump (booster) leads and trickle charging

Irregular usage or a weak battery may mean that a boost via jump (booster) leads, either from another vehicle or a portable boost pack is required to start the engine. A few words of warning:

• Before any form of external charging, check that the electrolyte level is correct (not sealed batteries). Remember, the electrolyte is highly corrosive sulphuric acid; very harmful to your health as well as your car if spilled. Do not breathe in fumes or allow electrolyte to make contact with skin. A charging battery will give off hydrogen gas, this is highly flammable. More modern-type batteries are sealed for life to protect us from these dangers.

• Be absolutely certain to attach the cables using the correct polarity (red cable to positive (+) first); double-check before making each connection. Do not rely on someone else on the other end of the cables – it is your responsibility to be sure that the connections are correct and your liability if not.

• During connection do not allow the cable clamps to accidentally touch any part of the vehicle, other than the intended part.

• Connect to the casualty vehicle first as the low charge battery may give off gas. Any arcing as the connection is made could cause an ignition that you most certainly do not want! It is both safer and more effective to make the earth (ground) connection to the casualty vehicle via a good earthing point on the engine, clear of moving parts, rather than the battery. This will reduce the number of interfaces, and potential voltage drops, between the battery terminal and the engine. The rescue vehicle should then be started and run at approximately 1500rpm to obtain maximum generator output. It's pointless to use a higher speed as the maximum current output is regulated at around this rpm.

• Allow the casualty battery to accept some charge for a few minutes, then switch off the donor engine before operating the casualty's starter. Once the casualty engine starts, very carefully remove the cables one at a time (negative first from both vehicles), again, being very careful not to allow the clamps to touch anything as you go.

• You may decide to trickle charge a flat battery before attempting to start the engine. A trickle charger places only a small current flow into the battery, and thus takes a considerable time to recover a low-charged battery. A fully flat battery can take up to 24 hours, but a partly-charged battery may take just a fraction of the time.

• The battery may give off hydrogen gas when being charged. Ensure that no means of ignition is anywhere near a battery being charged. Again, check the polarity of the charger connections and only switch on the charger once the connections have been made to eliminate any chance of arcing.

• Do not forget that your battery is on charge; check the charger ammeter periodically (this may be a row of lights on some) to ascertain the state of charging rate.

3. Battery acid spillage

Hidden behind the heater unit, it is all too easy to ignore the state of the battery with regard to spillage. The battery should stand in a plastic spill tray to prevent any acid from attacking the steel platform beneath. Ensure the tray is present and free from cracks or other damage. Acid vapour can also attack the bulkhead panel behind the battery. I recommend fitting a piece of rubber between the battery and bulkhead, with the edge of the rubber sitting inside the spill tray.

4. Battery security

The battery must be secured with the proper steel strap and J-bolts. Although sandwiched between the heater unit and bulkhead, this is not sufficient security to prevent the battery from moving sideways or upward. Should the car overturn, the terminals of an unsecured battery could short circuit against the bonnet, and should fuel vapour then escape from the carburettors – well, you can guess the rest ...

Ensure the battery is properly secured, and check regularly for any acid spillage and resultant corrosion. Hidden behind the heater unit, and with the low bonnet (hood) clearance, it tends to be overlooked. Ensure the plastic spill tray is fitted and not cracked.

The Lucas dynamo requires a periodic squirt of oil in the rear cover (arrowed) to lubricate the rear bearing. Only this and the brushes are common items to replace after a high mileage. The dynamo can be re-polarised to suit either positive or negative earth.

5. Charging system

The dynamo or alternator must produce a higher voltage than the battery voltage in order to keep the battery charged. The ignition light will illuminate when the charging voltage is below that of the battery voltage. However, even when the light is extinguished, there is no indication of the amount of current (amperage) being produced by the charging system. When the system is loaded with lights, windscreen wipers, heater fan, plus any other electrical accessories, the charging system must provide a sufficient current to maintain a charge to the battery. This is where a traditional ammeter is very useful in seeing how much current is flowing, and in which direction. This instrument was never fitted by the manufacturer, but is really useful on cars of this era which are prone to electrical maladies through ageing. Therefore, I recommend fitting an ammeter if you are unsure of how reliably the electrical system is performing (unless you are absoutely confident of your ability, have an electrician make the connections). The ammeter will help determine if a sluggish

An alternator produces a higher current at a lower engine speed than a dynamo, and requires no maintenance. A swap from dynamo to alternator is quite straightforward, but the earthing (grounding) must be changed to negative. Do not over-tension the fanbelt as this will strain the bearings for both dynamo and alternator.

A noticeable discharge reading whilst the engine is running above idling speed indicates that the charging system has a fault. An ammeter should maintain a reading of around +2 amps when the battery is fully charged. A brief reading of +15 to 20 amps will be seen following start up. An ammeter for an alternator-equipped vehicle will have a scale of +50 to -50.

starter is the product of a tired battery, an under-performing charging circuit, or even the starter itself.

Note that if you suspect a current drain when the car is not in use, a multimeter set to 10 amps range (bridging between the disconnected negative (-) cable and the negative battery post) or a modern current clamp will measure the drain more precisely.

6. Common modifications

Many owners convert the early positive earth (ground) versions to the later negative earth standard. This is usually to enable the fitting of present day electrical accessories, particularly in-car entertainment or power take off for satellite navigation, phone chargers, etc. Also, many owners who have experienced problems with the dynamo and voltage regulator ditch this, and fit an alternator which is negative earth only. A voltage regulator is not required with an alternator, but is sometimes left in place as a convenient means of retaining existing terminal connections rather than using block connectors. The function of the regulator must be isolated from the wiring in this instance. Additional lighting, an electric engine cooling fan, electronic ignition and alarm systems are typical of items that many owners fit. However, such additions are sometimes fitted very poorly, leading to problems that can affect the whole system. If faults become difficult to trace, it is often worth while disconnecting all additions to the system as a starting point.

7. Changing earth (ground) polarity

There is more to changing from positive to negative earth than just swapping the battery cables between terminals. If a dynamo is retained, this must be re-polarised. The electric rev counter is polarity sensitive and must be changed accordingly. The low tension connections to the coil must be transposed in order to

The two-bobbin voltage regulator (1) and fusebox (2) are mounted on the inner wing on the Sprite MkI only. The electrical contacts are susceptible to corrosion in this location. The fuse holder blades for the two fuses can corrode. A good place to start looking when the electrics play up.

All subsequent Spridgets with a dynamo had the voltage regulator (1) mounted on the bulkhead. Alternator-equipped examples dispensed with the regulator. The fusebox (2) was now mounted alongside the battery.

maintain full high tension voltage. And if an ammeter is fitted, swap the connections over. The early two-bobbin voltage regulator can accept a change of polarity, whilst the three-bobbin regulator was only introduced after the swap to negative earth. These can be retained regardless of polarity, but must be isolated or removed if changing to an alternator. Before you ask, the heater blower motor will continue to blow (not suck) regardless of polarity. Likewise, the electric fuel pump will not drain the carburettors to re-fill the tank!

8. Charging faults

If the battery is known to be in good condition yet fails to keep a sufficient charge, either the charging circuit is faulty or there is a drain on the electrical system somewhere.

The workshop manual describes the checks that can be made on the dynamo or alternator. The dynamo brushes will wear away after prolonged use but are easy to replace, check also that the armature is not badly worn. The rear bearing is a plain phosphor bronze bush which will also wear if not lubricated

The later three-bobbin regulator (1) and four-fuse circuit fusebox (2). If an early version has had the dynamo replaced by a regulator, this is often retained to act as a connections terminal, but with the regulator function removed or isolated.

9. General electrical faults

Poor or corroded earth connections are common on older vehicles. In time, spade, screw or bullet connections can all suffer corrosion. As most connectors are sheathed within a rubber sleeve, inspection is a matter of pulling each one apart. The bullet connectors behind the radiator grille are particularly prone to corrosion as they are constantly bombarded by whatever the road and weather conditions have in store. The fuse holders can also corrode and break down under load. Any item not functioning needs to be checked with a multimeter to ensure that both feed and earthing circuits are complete. If the circuit to a component is sound, then the component itself may have failed. With vehicles of this age, anything you would not normally expect

periodically, or if the fanbelt is over-tightened. A screeching sound from the rear cover of the dynamo may be heard when the bearing is dry or badly worn. A faulty voltage regulator will require replacement. Many owners decide this is a good time to change from a dynamo/voltage regulator system to an alternator and swap the polarity to negative earth as required. Essentially, if in good condition, the dynamo/regulator system is both reliable and quite sufficient to cope with the electrical needs of a standard specification Spridget. Before replacing any items, check that all earth and main battery connections are in good order. The body to engine earth connection underneath the car is often overlooked and can become damaged.

Bullet-type connectors can corrode unnoticed. The connectors behind the radiator grille are particularly vulnerable, as they face the elements full-on.

Check the cleanliness of bulb holder contacts and bulbs. The centre contact in the holder is spring-loaded: ensure that this moves freely.

could happen. Windscreen wiper motor, heater blower motor, switches and instruments can all life expire. Poorly earthing lamp units may cause some peculiar effects, especially the rear lamps. A bulb that fails to earth properly may find an earth (ground) through a twin filament bulb, such as the combined side lamp/ brake light bulb. Check all the lights, both singularly and with all the combinations of functions. A poor earth may result in some strange behaviour of neighbouring light circuits. Check that the bulb and bulb holder contacts are clean and the spring-loaded contact is moving freely within the centre of the holder.

10. Starter motor

The starter motor draws a very heavy current from the battery; all connections must be in good order to prevent a loss of power. If the starter motor labours when a fully charged battery is applied, then this may be due to worn armature brushes or a faulty starter solenoid. If the engine has been modified to a larger capacity or a higher compression ratio, then this will require more effort from the starter and battery to turn the flywheel. A pre-engaged starter motor was never fitted on any versions, so ensure that the bendix gear engages and disengages properly, the main spring can break. Over time, both the bendix and flywheel ring gears can become worn. Should the starter disengage before the engine fires, this may be the reason.

11. Instruments

Standard type Smiths-supplied instruments were used on all versions,excluding the Midget MkI (GAN1) only. For this application, the instruments were marked as being Jaegar, although they were still made by Smiths. Over the years, many minor variations occurred, and it is therefore important when replacing any instruments to ensure that you order the correct item. The manufacturer's part number is printed on the face of most instruments as the reference. Rev counters and fuel gauges are polarity sensitive so take this into account if the polarity has been changed. Speedometers must be correctly calibrated to the final drive ratio, so if the differential gear set has been changed to a different ratio, the speedometer will need to be changed as well. Speedometers are all cable-driven and, in time, can give a fluctuating reading. This may be caused by a worn or faulty cable but if a replacement does not cure this, then the speedometer may need to be changed. The trip distance (odometer) function is prone to failing. Speedometer and rev counters can loose correct calibration so investigate any readings that seem at odds. A quick check may be made by comparing the road speed per 1000rpm,

The rev counter is cable-driven from a gearbox on the rear of the dynamo on all 948cc engine versions. Torque wind-up in the cable during a gearchange can cause the needle to jump or flick. Do not confuse this rapid high reading with a slipping clutch. It has certainly fooled some owners into

The 948cc versions have a cable-driven rev counter from a small gearbox on the rear of the dynamo. A slipping fanbelt or damaged cable will provide inaccurate and unsteady readings. The cable can twist with a sudden fluctuation in engine speed; don't confuse this with clutch slip when changing gear. The cable and gearbox should only be lightly tightened.

Elderly instruments can give inaccurate and fluctuating readings. Speedo and rev counter (tachometer) readings can be compared in top gear in relation to the known speed per 1000rpm. Compare this to a sat nav speed reading, otherwise you may not know if either, or even both, instrument is at fault.

which varied in production according to final drive ratio and may be found in contemporary road tests. Non-original tyre sizes will also affect the calibration and accuracy of the speedometer. With original tyres fitted, the speed per 1000rpm for each of the three final drive ratios should be as follows.

4.22:1	Speed per 1000rpm	15.37mph (24.6kph)
3.90:1	Speed per 1000rpm	16.5mph (26.5kph)
3.72:1	Speed per 1000rpm	17.9mph (28.6kph)

Below: Great care is required when handling the temperature gauge capillary tube. The gauge and tube must be replaced as a unit if damaged. Early versions with the sender in the vertical flow radiator only give a reading after the thermostat has opened from cold, while later versions with the crossflow radiator have the sender placed beneath the thermostat in the cylinder head, the latter producing a reading prior to the thermostat opening. The cross flow radiator was not designed to incorporate the sender tube.

Above: The oil pressure gauge is generally very reliable, but the capillary tube for the temperature gauge is easily damaged. There is no oil pressure warning light to draw your attention to impending disaster, so keep a regular eye on the gauge. The light above the gauge will illuminate should the oil filter bypass valve open.

thinking that the clutch was losing its grip. Fluctuating readings can be due to drive cable faults, or a very loose fanbelt causing a slippage of the dynamo pulley.

The combined oil pressure/temperature gauge is normally reliable, but the capillary tubing leading from the radiator (vertical flow

radiator) or cylinder head (crossflow radiator) is easily damaged. Once broken or cracked, the complete gauge and attached capillary tube must be replaced. This can be a tricky job when trying to feed the tubing through the dashboard and engine compartment without incurring damage to the tube. The Midget lost the oil pressure gauge from GAN6-200001 (August 1977) to leave an electrically operated temperature gauge.

The fuel gauge can give inaccurate readings, most likely this will be the result of a faulty tank sender unit or a poor earthing of the fuel tank. The tank will have to be removed to access the sender unit in the top face of the tank. The tank earths (grounds) via the mounting studs but corrosion, or a new tank with too thick a coat of paint, may prevent conductivity. Positive earth versions have no damping effect of the fuel gauge needle; a certain amount of needle flicker may be expected as the fuel sloshes around in the tank. Negative earth versions used a voltage stabiliser in the circuit to damp out sudden movements of the needle.

Some owners can never have too much information – hopefully a wiring diagram, too. No doubt a pilot's licence, as well as a driver's licence, is required for this car!

The original soft top and tonneau cover were made from ICI Vynide material, with Vybak for the windows. The seats and trim panels were also covered with a Vynide material. Rubber floor matting was used until the introduction of the Sprite MkII (HAN7) and Midget MkI (GAN2) in October 1962, after which carpeting was fitted. Almost all trim items are currently available, the main exception being the rubber floor matting. The soft top was

Owners of early versions have plenty to keep them occupied when there is a change in the weather. An abundance of bags, covers and frames provide a sort of automotive camping experience. Ensure you have it all before you set off.

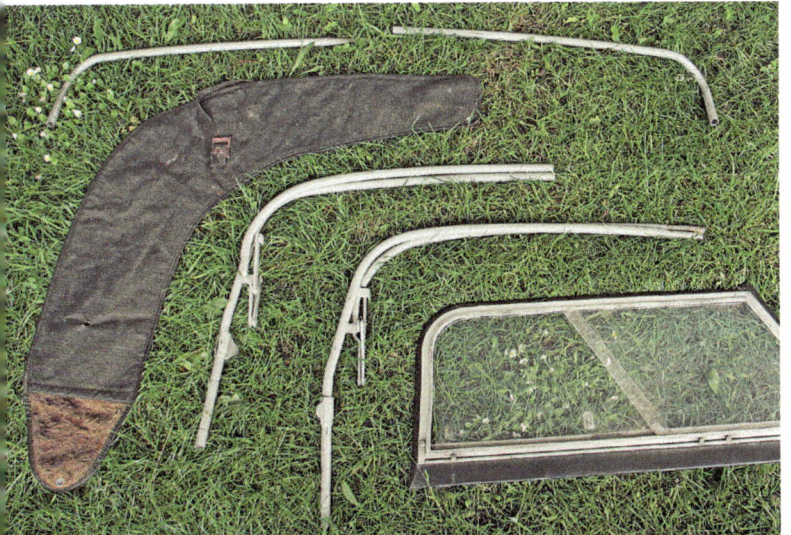

originally placed over a detachable tubular steel frame; with the introduction of the 1275cc versions, the soft top and frame were attached to the car, and folded into an enlarged space behind the seats. Detachable aluminium frame side screens containing sliding Perspex windows were replaced by fully winding windows in March 1964. It should be noted that, unless the optional hard top was ordered, the very early Sprite MkI was equipped with fabric side screens with Vybak windows on a steel frame.

1. Common problems

Any tears in the weather equipment and interior trim will be obvious. However, regular inspection may reveal that a small area of damage can be repaired before becoming a major concern. When a soft top or tonneau cover becomes badly torn, replacement is the only sensible option. Weather equipment in poor condition will not only allow increased wind noise, but let in rain as well. This will then have the knock-on effect of damaging the interior trim and soaking the carpets; if left untreated, rust will then spread across the floor. There are safety implications, too: should a soft top rip away from the fasteners at speed, this can present a real danger to yourself and other road users. The soft top, tonneau cover and body-fitted fasteners should be regularly inspected for security. In time, the Vybak windows can become opaque, whereupon they can be removed and new ones sewn in by a specialist upholsterer. Cleaning products are available for opaque Vybak windows, but replacement is generally the more effective solution. Fabric fasteners, such as 'Tenax' and 'Lift the dot' can be replaced, too, and some minor damage may be

When a soft top is in this sort of condition, replacement is essential. You can do this job yourself, but to do it properly requires care and patience. Obtaining the correct soft top tension and getting all the fasteners into the correct positions should not be rushed.

Water in Spridgets can come from below as well as above. Rust holes in the floors and sills will rot the carpet from below. Remove carpets regularly to check underneath for damp and corrosion.

repairable. New tonneau zips can be fitted but always compare repair costs against buying a new item. In general, replacing trim items to original specification is not expensive. Some owners prefer to upgrade to leather or double duck materials, along with the associated increase in cost.

2. Carpets

Carpets are usually laid under the seat runners and cannot be removed without first removing the seats. In other areas the carpets may be held in place with adhesive. Sodden carpets are therefore not easily removed in order to dry out properly. Nasty smells and corrosion forming on the floorpan will be the price to pay. Ensure, then, that all of the carpeting can be quickly and easily removed for drying out and cleaning when required. The

Carpets that retain damp will rot out the floors in time. Ordinarily, the seat will have to be removed to free the carpet. Cut it around the seat runners and it can easily be pulled out for regular drying and inspection.

carpet can be cut so as to slot around the seat runners, whilst none of the floor carpeting actually needs to be glued into place.

3. Seats

Seats fitted before August 1965 have a lift-out sponge Dunlopillo-supported cushion fitted within a steel base frame. The steel base of the cushion can rust from moisture transferred from wet carpeting. The sponge padding can also soak up moisture and deteriorate eventually; a musty smell may become very apparent. Seats from August 1965 onwards have a thicker backrest; the

The early-type seat with cushions removable from the seat frame, making it easy to retrieve 'lost' items. Not so after August 1965, when the complete seat had to be removed to retrieve those small coins. Note the optional 'rear seat' cushion. Very rare to find today, few customers believed that a Spridget could ever seriously be a four-seater by ordering this option!

cushion is attached to the base frame and must be removed from the car for inspection. These have a rubber diaphragm base, the steel support hooks can tear away from the diaphragm in time. If the cushion feels very spongy and low, then this may be the problem. From 1969, reclining backrests were provided, and headrests fitted as standard to some export versions. Headrests were an option on home market versions.

4. Trim panels

Side liner panels can warp with age but are generally easily replaced. Always exercise care when removing the door liner panels. The spring retaining clips can easily rip out of the panel.

5. Windscreen (windshield)

The windscreen is mounted within an alloy frame. If a damaged windscreen cannot be dealt with in situ, it will need to be replaced. The early 'non-door handle' versions have four screws holding the frame which can be easily accessed from the outside of the vehicle. However, the front screws can corrode into the captive nuts and may need to be very carefully drilled out. 'Door handle' versions need to have the dashboard removed or dropped to access the securing screws. Dismantling the frame can be very awkward as the screws often seize and must be drilled out. Assembly can be equally difficult, as the rubber seals take a lot of compressing to allow the frame to seat into position. Some windscreen repair companies may be reluctant to replace a windscreen; it can be long and tricky job. Expect a bill to match!

6. Windscreen wipers

Sluggishly operating wipers may be due to a worn motor or, more likely a partially seized or damaged cable linking the motor to the scuttle mounted wheel boxes. Should the motor appear

The windscreen frame must be removed to replace the glass. The forward screw on 'non-door handle' versions can prove very difficult to extract. Drilling-out may be the only course – very carefully, though.

The frame must also be removed on 'door handle' versions to replace the glass. Now, however, the dashboard must be dropped to gain access to the forward retaining nut. Replace the lower sealing rubber as a matter of course. Note: three windscreen wipers for the North American versions from 1968.

to be labouring and attempting to move on the mountings, this may indicate that the cable has become stiff to move within the outer tube. The cable may produce some noise with the motor sounding strained and running hot. Removing the cable and wheel boxes requires dropping the dashboard to gain access. Sloppy wipers arms may be due to worn wheel boxes. The wheel box driven gear can be rotated to an unworn segment of the gear, thus restoring some further service, but if the cable teeth are worn this may only provide a temporary fix.

7. Hardtops

An optional factory hard top was a very popular addition when these cars were in normal daily usage. As well as factory hard tops, there were many aftermarket versions in a variety of different styles. The quality, fit and practicality was varied. If you have a hard top, or are looking to purchase one, ensure that it is the correct one for your model. It is essential that it fits snugly and securely. Check that it fits all the way around and that all the attachments are present and working securely. Check the

Many different designs of hardtop were available, and various changes to how they were fitted were made in the earlier years of production. With the introduction of the 1275cc versions in late 1966, fitment of the hardtop remained unchanged until the end of production. Ensure your car has the correct fitment for its version, and that all securing devices are present and effective.

An earlier hardtop that, at first glance, looks rather attractive.

A closer look shows extensive cracking in the fibreglass construction. This one could be beyond saving.

condition of all sealing rubbers. It can be very difficult to track down replacement catches and sealing rubbers for some hard tops. Check for cracking of the fibreglass construction and that securing catches are not about to break away.

14 Bodywork

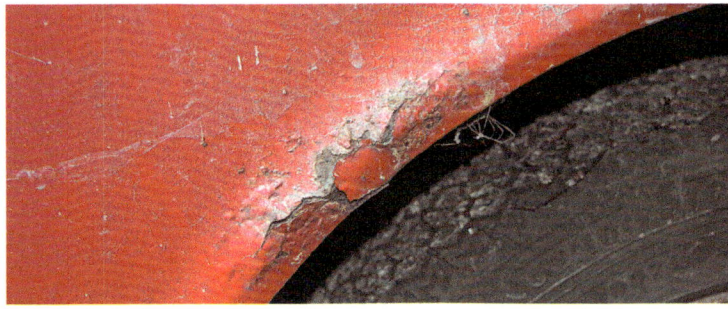

The Sprite and Midget were the first mass-produced sports cars to have a monocoque, or unitary, constructed bodyshell unit. That is to say that there was no separate chassis or any subframes to carry the major mechanical components. Everything is bolted to the main bodyshell unit. Although this provides a very strong and lightweight means of construction, the many box sections that make up the monocoque to provide this strength are also rather prone to moisture retention and corrosion attack.

1. Common problems
Corrosion, accident damage and poor quality repairs can seriously affect the strength and safety of the monocoque.

Even a small amount of 'surface' rust is just the tip of an iceberg. The corrosion around this wheelarch will be an expensive job to repair properly.

Doors that fail to shut or don't fit properly are sure signs that the bodyshell is out of alignment. All body panels should fit neatly with parallel and even gap lines. All hinges for opening panels must be in good order, along with locks and catches to secure these in both open and closed positions. Bubbling in the paintwork is an early indication that rust is forming from behind the panel; this will be just the tip of the iceberg and must not be ignored.

2. Misalignment
A bodyshell may display obvious signs of misalignment with uneven and tapering gaps between various panels. However, even if the panel fit appears to be good, there could still be

Only the lower edges of a Spridget will rust, generally from the floor up to the base of the windscreen. So check everywhere!

This door fits nicely in line with the door pillar, but is way out, top-to-bottom, at the trailing edge. If the door is not twisted, then something far more serious is out of alignment. No amount of hinge adjustment will rectify this.

hidden misalignment problems lower down. This may be due to previous accident damage. Begin with the front crossmember structure; this carries the front suspension and steering components. Look very carefully all around this area for any

signs of wrinkling, cracks, non-original welding and repairs. The main floorpan could have developed a slight twist as the result of a severe accident or very poor repairs to a severely corroded floorpan structure. This may cause a misalignment between front and rear suspension attachment points. A car that does not maintain a straight course, with a bias to drift left or right, needs to be checked out. Remember, tyre problems, sticking brakes or worn suspension could also be the cause, so eliminate these items first. As a useful check, find a clear and safe space, drive around slowly on full steering lock, and release the steering wheel. Does the steering self-centre equally from both left and right locks? An example that displays a steering bias for no apparent reason needs to be properly checked on an alignment jig. Should an alignment check show a discrepancy, then a new bodyshell, if available for your model, may prove a better solution, rather than attempting to realign a damaged item.

3. Modifications

Many Sprite MkIs lost their original one-piece rear-hinging bonnet (hood) assembly as a result of accident or corrosion damage. Also, some owners may simply have wanted to personalise their Sprite by substituting a fibreglass bonnet, either to the original pattern to reduce weight, or for one of many alternative designs which became very popular. Most aftermarket bonnets were hinged at the front to improve access and provide a simpler and safer means of attachment. Some bonnets had a very small radiator air intake that could compromise engine cooling. Some aftermarket bonnets fitted quite well, depending on the resourcefulness of the person fitting it, but others required much fettling before a reasonable fit could be obtained, if indeed at all. Most relied on external straps to fasten the rear lower edge of the bonnet wings to the sills. These could be rubber straps or over-centre type catches.

part of the engine, as clearance is small (it is also small on the original bonnet).

Later versions can also have a fibreglass bonnet and wings fitted, as all of the front end panels can simply be unbolted. Again, this can be a one-piece bonnet of original or alternative style. Separate wings and bonnet made to the original pattern can replace the standard steel items to save weight, or as a cheaper means of repairing damaged or rusty panels. Fibreglass sills were available at one time but, if fitted as a direct replacement on their own, these seriously compromise the structural strength of the car. A complete fibreglass rear shroud is available for the Sprite MkI but this must be fitted properly. More drastic changes to original appearance can be made by the fitting of Lenham or Arkley conversions which, again, must be done properly. Always check the way non-original panels or assemblies have been fitted. Structural strength and safety can seriously be compromised if this has not been expertly carried out. Currently, a kit is available to convert later versions to Sprite MkI appearance, using fibreglass front and rear mouldings. Although changing the front is a simple enough job, with little effect on the integrity of the main structure, the rear end must be done very carefully and properly.

4. Additions

The addition of a roll-over bar is a popular choice for owners who want to be safe on the road in an open-top car and, indeed, it is mandatory for any form of motorsport. Many types of roll bar are available, but an item for use in motorsport must conform to current regulations covering the sport. As before, the method of fitting is all important, and must be fully checked. A roll bar footing on a corroded floor, or one that is not secured properly, will not perform as you might expect if put to the test! Some roll

One of the most popular re-bodied conversions, the Arkley. Replacement front and rear bodywork in fibreglass give the Spridget a completely different look. Only the doors, windscreen and sills provide a clue to what's beneath. Still available today.

The fitting of a fibreglass bonnet does not really affect structural strength of the monocoque; however, your insurers should be informed of such a modification. Fibreglass bonnets are considerably lighter but can vibrate and cause rubbing and squeaking noises if not very carefully fitted. Some may contact

A roll-over bar is a popular addition. There are many different types, but in each case, it must be fitted properly and safely. A full roll cage provides ultimate safety, but may also prove difficult to live with in a car used every day.

bars may also hamper seatbelt and seat adjustment operations, and make entry and exit from the seat more difficult.

5. Annoying squeaks and rattles

A good Sprite or Midget should be pleasantly free from such noises. However, any noises that do become apparent should be investigated to confirm whether this is simply an annoyance, or something more serious is amiss. The bodyshell should not suffer anything more than very slight flexing under normal driving conditions. A slight tremor may be felt by placing a finger at the top of the door to scuttle gap; anything more than slight may reveal a weakening of the bodyshell. A door that produces a rattling at the catch may simply be poorly adjusted, suffering from worn hinges, or far more seriously, the sign of a weakened bodyshell.

The bonnet can also rattle, more so with the Sprite MkI, this being a large and rather flexible structure. The absence of the rubber buffer blocks on the inner wing tops and sills may aggravate this. A seating rubber along the scuttle should support the rear edge of the bonnet (hood) when closed. Later versions just had rubber buffer blocks along the drip channels, but check the edges of the bonnet for any signs of rubbing against the surrounding metalwork. If the gap lines around the bonnet are too tight or uneven following panel replacement, then you may be able to slacken the front wing securing bolts and ease the wing panel clear. If not, then either the wing panel or bodyshell unit may be at fault. Likewise, the boot lid should sit on rubber buffers in the drip rail and a surrounding weather-sealing rubber.

6. Hinges

The door hinges can wear, particularly if not lubricated occasionally. This can lead to uneven door gaps and shut problems. The hinges are adjustable for initial fit but any wear should be corrected by replacement or repair. The bonnet hinges allow for some adjustment of the bonnet panel, but beware of

The pressed steel bonnet (hood) hinges can distort and crack at the bottom of the U-shape, especially given the heavy Sprite MkI bonnet. Although adjustment is provided, once a hinge loses its shape it should be replaced. The dashboard has to be dropped to gain access to the hinge bolt. North American versions used a different hinge from 1968: a much stronger design that can be replaced without disturbing the dashboard.

damaged hinges, particularly with the Sprite MkI. The pressed steel hinges can distort and develop cracks under the heavy weight of the bonnet. This is less of a problem on later versions, but not unknown. The dashboard has to be removed to gain

Try lifting the rear edge of the door to check for wear in the hinges. The hinges are provided with adjustment for initial door alignment but, if worn, should be replaced. A drop of oil will prolong life. Ensure the fabric check strap is in good order; if the wind catches the door it can mean a big repair to door and door pillar.

access to the pivot bolt, so changing a hinge is not a quick job. From December 1968, North American versions used a cantilever type bonnet hinge as a safety revision. The boot lid hinges carry far less weight and generally last well but, again, check condition and adjustment if the panel gap is uneven.

7. Catches and locks

All opening panels should shut easily and securely against their corresponding catches. Adjustment is provided, but once set correctly upon initial assembly, no further adjustment should be required. A door that pops off the catch when driving may just have a badly worn catch or hinges. However, excessive flexing of the bodyshell may exacerbate this. Door catches post-March 1964 are of the anti-burst design and should not allow the door to pop open. Conversely, sticking or dragging catches, preventing an easy door release, may be due to poor initial adjustment, worn hinges or a misaligned bodyshell.

The 'non-door handle' door catch on the B post. Check for any wear or damage to the cone-shaped projection. If this is worn, or should the bodyshell be out of alignment or suffer excessive flexing, then the door can 'self' open.

From March 1964, an anti-burst door latch was fitted. Check for rubbing from an incorrectly adjusted door fit or body misalignment.

The bonnet hood must latch down securely at the front. The Sprite MkI has expanding locking rods that must engage fully in the locking plate holes on each of the frame rails. Never drive the car if the rods are not engaged. The later versions have a conventional locking arrangement in the slam panel, the cable release should be lubricated regularly to prevent seizure and cable breakage. Both types of bonnet have a secondary safety latch: check that this is working and lubricated periodically.

The Sprite MkI lacked exterior door handles and locks, and even a boot lid. Later versions, with such luxuries included, need to be checked for the correct operation of all handles and locks. Locks can fail, and replacements require a new key. As new, the same key operated the doors and boot locks, so any replacement may mean a further key for your key ring.

8. Exterior fittings

Chrome-plated items will deteriorate with age but are easily replaced. An owner has the choice whether to replace with new or to have an original item re-chromed. Certainly, there have been quality issues with the fit and durability of some new items. Re-plating, if done properly, will at least solve the fit issue and most likely provide a better quality and longer lasting finish. However, this is not usually the cheapest option in the short term , though it may prove to be in the longer term. Always look after chromed details with careful cleaning and protecting if the car is out of use for long periods. Radiator grilles are available new for all versions, as are most badges (the most notable exception being

As nice as chrome looks when new, it does not stay that way. Keep it clean as best you can. The choice here is whether to buy new, or re-chrome an old item. If saveable, the latter option may prove better in the long run.

the Austin Sprite (AAN10) badges. With only 1022 examples built, and probably only 10% of those surviving, the badge makers may feel the market is too small to reproduce the grille and boot badges).

9. Looking after the body

Maintaining the exterior appearance by regular cleaning and waxing is obvious enough. The real danger lurks from within. Regardless of the annual MoT test (UK) or other safety test, the examiner can only check that which is visible. However it is within the many box sections and behind the trim and carpets that the problems begin. At least once a year, remove as much of the trim and carpeting as you can to examine the exposed metalwork. This will also allow access to wax inject the box sections and cavities through the apertures that are otherwise hidden from view. Remove all rubber blanking plugs and inject a good quality spraying rust preventative. Some owners will drill additional access holes to ensure that all box sections are fully injected. This must be done thoughtfully of course– do not drill holes unless you understand the construction of the car. Plug any additional holes with grommets.

Clear any mud traps regularly, especially the gap between the front wing and sill; a thin piece of card or plastic will help to dislodge any debris. Also, ensure the drain hole at the base of the triangular aperture behind the front wheels is clear. With quarter-elliptic rear suspension, debris can build up in the spring box around the spring. A dust shield was introduced to reduce this, and can easily be made up if missing. This is not so much a problem with the semi-elliptic springs, but still check for debris build-up anyway. The front edge of the post MkI bonnet is a real rust trap. The box section traps water in large quantities. Additional drain holes, or slots, will overcome most of this and provide better access for wax injection.

Right: The drain hole at the bottom triangular aperture behind the front wheel is easily overlooked. If this becomes blocked, the cavity will fill with debris and eventually lead to serious corrosion problems. This is a critical structural area, so check regularly.

From October 1969, the radiator grille was commonised between Midget and Sprite; only the badge differentiated. Based on the cheaper Sprite grille, black now replaced a bright finish.

Much patchwork welding around the rear bulkhead and spring location area of this Sprite MkI. This is a highly stressed area: the longitudinal top-hat section transfers loading from the rear spring along the floor to the jacking point crossmember in front of the seats.

The front edge of the bonnet/hood (except Sprite MkI) is a notorious rust haven. The box section harbours moisture. Additional drain holes are a good idea and provide better access for rust inhibitor to be sprayed in. A repair front section is available, but not always a good long-term solution, as a crack can form where this is joined in.

A rust hole behind the front wheel can cause problems. The footwell, front floor, inner and outer sills will all suffer attack from water ingress. Check regularly for any water penetration opportunities within the wheelarches and floors.

For many owners, their Spridget is not their front line vehicle. It is kept for when the weather, a special event or the mood suggests that it's time to go out and have some fun. As such, many Spridgets are not in regular usage and may spend time waiting in the garage or in storage until the time is right. Just like us, cars thrive on regular exercise and periods of slumber can bring about problems of their own. If your Spridget is to give reliable service and remain in good condition, then there are some points to be considered. If your car is parked up and in danger of getting bored with sitting around, then the following tips may help:

1. Battery
Many owners fit a battery master switch, or link, to easily isolate the battery from the electrical circuit. This not only prevents a

A clue here about infrequent use: if the switch gear and controls display a lack of use, will whatever they operate be in any better condition?

discharge should there be a live circuit with the ignition turned off, but it may also prevent some serious damage if a short circuit occurs through a damp or condensation-promoted short circuit.

2. Hydraulic fluid
Ordinary mineral-based hydraulic fluid is hydroscopic, which means it can absorb moisture. Although fluid should be changed at regular intervals, the build-up of moisture can still cause corrosion attack within the system. By using a silicon hydraulic fluid, the hydraulic system can be safely protected from corrosive attack over very long periods. The two types of fluid are incompatible and must not be mixed.

3. Exhaust system
A mild steel exhaust system will quietly corrode away from the inside, even when not in use. A stainless steel system should last forever, and some manufacturers include a life time guarantee on their products.

4. Brakes
Never store the car for long periods with the handbrake applied. The rear brake linings can become stuck to the brake drums. Use chocks under the wheels to prevent your Spridget wandering off. Wheel cylinders are prone to sticking with inactivity, so check that the brakes apply and release properly before venturing out. The bare metal friction faces within the brake drum of the front brake disc will soon corrode and cause the friction material to stick. Even when freed off, the layer of corrosion will reduce braking

A mild steel exhaust system can just as easily rust away with age as usage. The transverse rear silencer is particularly prone to corrosion. Replacing with a stainless steel system makes a lot of sense.

performance until worn off. The first few applications of the brakes may be very ineffective and very noisy until most of the corrosion build-up is worn away.

5. Clutch

The clutch pressure plate can seize to the flywheel when left for extended periods. Ordinarily, after warming the engine, the grip can be broken. With the engine turned off, wheels chocked, select top gear, apply the handbrake fully, depress the clutch and operate the starter. The sudden torque input is usually enough to jolt the clutch free. If your Spridget is stored long-term, it is highly advisable to operate all the controls at regular intervals to keep the moving parts free.

6. Engine

Once a fortnight the engine should be run up to operating temperature to ensure that everything remains well lubricated, and that cooling, fuel and electrical systems have some exercise. If it is envisaged that the engine may

An engine left as long as this must be carefully checked before attempting to start it. Add a few drops of oil down each sparkplug hole, and rotate by hand to ensure no tight spots – assuming it will turn at all, that is.

not be run for a very long time, change the oil and filter to ensure that the oil is free of contaminates. Also, squirt a small amount of engine oil down the sparkplug holes to lubricate the upper cylinder walls and piston rings. Do not overdo this; you do not want to risk hydraulic locking of the engine next time you do attempt a start-up. Any engine that has been left standing for a long time should be turned over by hand with the sparkplugs removed to ensure that it will rotate freely. With the plugs still removed operate the starter, and wait for the oil pressure to build to ensure that the system is primed before starting the engine.

7. Fuel system

The SU electric fuel pump does not always take kindly to long periods of inactivity. If you do not hear the characteristic clicking of the pump when the ignition is switched on, then do not expect the engine to run. Sometimes, just tapping the pump body with a hammer handle can awaken it. It is not very accessible; you will soon be considering a new pump or a modern type of pump that should not suffer this fault.

Despite a good tread depth, this tyre was left under-inflated for 15 years without being turned. The resultant flat spot and damage to the carcass will render it fit only for recycling. If long periods of inactivity are likely, raise the car off the ground to remove the load.

8. Tyres (Tires)

Tyres can develop flat spots if left stationary under load for prolonged periods of time, especially if under inflated. Always check tyre pressures regularly, but if a very long period of inactivity is envisaged, raise and support the car from the ground. This also allows the opportunity for the wheels to be rotated to help prevent corrosion build-up on the bare metal braking surfaces.

9. Before driving

Allow the engine to fully warm up before driving off. Check that all controls and electrical circuits are responding before venturing onto the road. As the engine warms, check tyre pressures, for leakages and strange noises.

From the very beginning, Sprites were modified for all types of motor sports and improved road use. The manufacturer offered a very comprehensive list of options, soon joined by various aftermarket companies offering their own special products and services. Whether just to personalise a Spridget with a few simple bolt-on goodies, or to modify for circuit racing or international rallying, few cars had previously been better catered for. The ensuing years saw even more options becoming available to tempt an owner, and this continues even today. If your ideal is a sports car designed over half a century ago but with a modern twin-cam, 16-valve fuel-injected engine driving through a 5-speed gearbox, then if you can afford it, you can have it.

A modified Spridget can still be a highly competitive car in motorsport and tremendous fun on the road, but only if modified thoughtfully and properly. In most cases, there will be side effects dependant upon the modifications carried out. Increased fuel consumption, increased maintenance, higher noise level, a harder ride and reduced reliability may be the penalties for an increase in performance. Your highly modified engine may prove to be reliable enough, but the greater strain on clutch, gearbox and rear axle can give rise to secondary problems. Furthermore, will the brakes and suspension be a match for

A single SU HIF carburettor and long centre branch tubular exhaust manifold are popular modifications for the A-series engine. Note the high temperature insulating wrap around the exhaust to reduce heat radiating to the carburettor.

that extra 50bhp or so? Rarely is a single modification enough to either satisfy an owner or produce a coherent update of the basic design. It can be a long and rocky road, even if international rallying is not your objective!

1. Think before you modify

As tempting as it is to modify your car, assess your starting point carefully. Shortcomings may simply be original components that are not in good health. Replacing worn shock absorbers, for example, may be all that you need to give the ride and handling that you desire without resorting to expensive and non-original

parts. Do you really need to fit larger carburettors to improve power if your engine is only running on three cylinders? A new set of HT leads may be all that is required to restore performance. Modifying a vehicle is never as simple as it first appears, so examine your starting point in relation to your ultimate objective; many owners fail to get to their objective as simply or within the time frame or budget they had envisaged.

2. Reliability

With a possible reduction in reliability or life of original components, new items may bring their own special problems. The fitting of the Rover K-series engine is a popular modification, providing performance that none of the original engines can match. However, this engine has a reputation for head gasket problems all of its own. On the other hand the popular modification of fitting a Ford 5-speed gearbox provides a far stronger, more reliable gearbox than any of the originals.

3. Servicing

The ease of servicing, availability of spare parts and advice for each and every variation of a modified example can be problematic. Any faults in the car may be unique to your own recipe of modifications. You may have to devise your own servicing schedule based on the advice from the various manufacturers and parts suppliers that you have used. You can also develop your own experience of the

Tuning an original engine will never be sufficient for some owners. A Rover K-series engine is a very popular choice, along with a Ford 5-speed gearbox. This lifts the Spridget into a whole new world. Brakes and suspension need to be uprated to cope with such an increase in power.

idiosyncrasies and needs of your particular creation as bits work loose, break or fall off.

4. Safety

Not only may you expect your modified Spridget to be the hottest in the region, but you will certainly want it to be reliable and safe too. There seems to be an enormous amount of regulatory freedom toward modified vehicles in some countries, but this is no excuse to ignore the responsibilities that go with modifying a car. A Rover K-series or Ford Zetec engine can easily provide well over 150bhp, but would anyone fit such an engine and still retain the front drum brakes of the earlier Spridgets?

5. Evolutionary modifications

Not all modifications are about improving performance or comfort. We have already seen that many owners replace original equipment as a means to improved reliability and serviceability. These sorts of modifications are all part of an evolutionary support from the industry to make life easier for the Spridget owner of today. Although some owners wish to maintain absolute originality of specification, perhaps in order to gain points at concours events, many others want to take advantage of these updates for practical reasons.

The following are typical of 'evolutionary' modifications:
• Stainless steel exhaust system
• Copper hydraulic pipes
• Silicone hydraulic fluid
• Brake servo
• Electronic fuel pump
• Crankshaft rear oil seal kit for A-series engines
• Ball bearing clutch release bearing for A-series engine
• Spin-on oil filter cartridge for pre-1970 A-series engines
• Alternators
• Electronic ignition
• Electric engine cooling fan
• Telescopic shock absorbers
• Electric windscreen washer pump

To take this a stage further, a 5-speed gearbox conversion has become a very popular modification, especially as there have been some quality and availability issues over reconditioned original gearboxes. Not only does a modern 5-speed gearbox provide a wider selection of gear ratios with better cruising ability, it can handle more power and last longer too! Another very popular modification is to replace the twin SU carburettors, as applied to the A-series engine, with a single SU HIF (horizontal, integral float). A special inlet manifold can be purchased to enable this. The HIF is a very efficient and simple unit that was widely used on later MG Rover vehicles. In hand with this, the original cast iron exhaust manifold is often discarded in favour of a tubular long centre branch (LCB) manifold.

More traditional common modifications concern air filters, steering wheel, roll bar and additional instruments and lighting. It should also be remembered that many earlier versions were updated by substituting components from later versions. To find a Sprite MkI with a 1098cc or 1275cc engine, gearbox and disc front brakes is not at all uncommon. Hence, a factory original specification Sprite or Midget can be very hard to find today.

6. Modifying for motorsport

First and foremost, obtain a copy of the rules governing the motorsport events that you have in mind. These will cover the safety items and permitted modifications with which your car must comply. A change of engine capacity, engine type, change of transmission or fibreglass, lightweight panels may not be allowed within certain categories. Join a club where members actively compete; here, you can learn a lot from their experiences. Learn from their mistakes before making your own – it can be cheaper and safer that way!

7. Modifying for road use

For road use, you have a very wide choice of things that can be modified. Before wading in, have a goal in mind. Do you want

to keep the main components that your version was built with, and modify them, or go the whole hog and replace with whatever you fancy? Swapping major components can cause all manner of secondary problems; again, it is well worth joining a club where you can benefit from the mistakes and successes that fellow modifiers have experienced. Setting a budget for modifying a

Spridgets enjoy a very active motorsport calendar. Destined only for circuit racing, this purpose-modified example is one of many in regular competition.

A very fine collection of period motorsport Spridgets at Burghley House to celebrate 50 years of the MG Midget in 2011. Some very famous examples that are very rarely, if ever, seen together at the same time.

A Rover V8 engine and Ford Sierra four-wheel drive system are in this Midget, and still there's room for two people. Just goes to show how far these cars can be modified.

car is very difficult, once you start, be prepared to keep on spending. Remember, whatever you decide, your car must still comply with local road vehicle regulations. It must be safe and manageable – following road users will not be impressed if your lowered suspension causes you to run aground on the first speed hump you encounter, nor will your neighbours if the exhaust noise disturbs their peace! An engine that goes like stink but cannot run below 3000rpm, oils the sparkplugs and overheats in traffic will not be fun for very long.

8. Rolling roads

Prototype engines destined for mass-production undergo many hours of development testing on a dynamometer to ensure that performance, efficiency and reliability targets are met. The basic settings are established as being optimum for that particular specification. Any form of modifying an engine away from the manufacturer's specification should, therefore, also be followed

Anti-tramp bar, telescopic rear shock absorber, and an uprated halfshaft are all readily available to cope with more power than any original Spridget left the factory with.

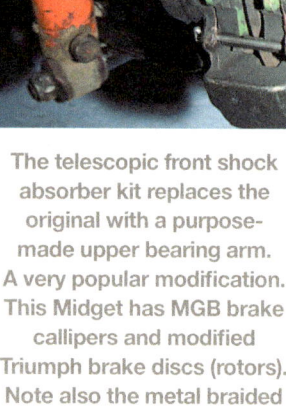

The telescopic front shock absorber kit replaces the original with a purpose-made upper bearing arm. A very popular modification. This Midget has MGB brake callipers and modified Triumph brake discs (rotors). Note also the metal braided hydraulic hose.

by some form of testing to ensure that the modifications are performing to the best advantage and safely. It is not practicable to use a bench test dynamometer for road vehicles, so a rolling road test is a very good and sensible alternative. It is pointless spending a huge amount of time and money modifying an engine and then not having it set

up correctly afterwards. Setting the fuel to air ratio and ignition systems correctly is vital, and not something that can be done properly without specialised equipment. If your Spridget has fuel injection and electronic ignition controlled from an electronic engine management system, then this will need to be remapped by a specialist in conjunction with a rolling road test where all parameters can be monitored accurately. Often, a session on a rolling road can be the best value for money tune-up around. Although a standard specification Spridget can be set up very well by a competent home mechanic, a session on a rolling road may reveal a few hidden horsepower, smoother running and better economy beyond the reach of even the best spanner and screwdriver!

Today, most motorists simply make do with a mobile phone, membership of a rescue service and a credit card to take care of any motoring mishaps. All very sensible of course, but should you think a little deeper into this? If you do call out one of the rescue services, the chances are that the technician may not have encountered a Midget or Sprite for a very long time, if indeed, ever before. Will they know that there is nowhere to plug in the diagnostic computer for example? Perhaps that is a little unkind, but your car is from another century after all. It is easy to become paranoid when selecting the quantity of spare parts and tools to carry with you on a journey. In reality, you do not have enough room to be prepared for every possible eventuality so a few basic items will have to suffice. If you do need to call for help, then your own knowledge of your Spridget and diagnostic skills should be of great help to a roadside rescue technician who may be totally unfamiliar with something that went out of production so many years ago.

What to carry with you

1. Tools

All the nuts and bolts are of UNF or UNC thread pattern with imperial across the flats (AF) head size. Hence, do not waste space by carrying a full socket set with either metric or BSW sizes. Similarly, Allen keys or Torx sets are just a waste of space. A few open-ended and ring spanners (wrenches) plus electrical, crosshead and flat blade screwdrivers, and a pair of pliers should take care of most things. Ensure you have all you need to change a road wheel, but do not rely on just the original side jack. A scissors jack is much safer to use. Carry a piece of timber to use

as a secure base and load spreader beneath the jack on uneven or soft ground.

2. Being towed

Having no power-assisted controls, then a direct tow behind another vehicle is possible. From the Sprite MkII and Midget MkI onwards, a towing bracket was fitted to each frame rail behind the front bumper. The Sprite MkI lacks this feature but brackets

A towing bracket is bolted to the front of both main frame rails. Although not fitted to the Sprite MkI, it is simple to retro-fit a bracket from the later versions. Never tow from any of the suspension or steering components.

can easily be fitted as per the later versions. Never tow from the suspension or steering components. Towing laws may vary so ensure you know the local and current laws before accepting a tow. A direct tow can be a frightening and risky experience; hence, the rescue services are by far the best and safest option.

3. Spares

Again, you do not have a lot of room to carry a bulky collection of spares. Ignition components such as a contact breaker set, condenser, rotor arm and perhaps a coil will not take up much room. Nor for that matter would a complete distributor unit. A fan belt and emergency thermostat by-pass hose for the A-series engine and a set of light bulbs and fuses can all be squeezed into the corner of the boot. Some owners carry a spare electric fuel pump, as an elderly SU pump can resign with very little notice. Anything more than this is not likely to be a quick roadside fix, so forget about carrying a spare clutch plate or halfshaft – if something like this fails, then its time for the mobile phone and rescue service.

4. General

Some very useful general items may include a length of electrical cable and a roll of insulation tape for any electrical by-pass surgery. Cable ties have endless uses, and you may also find a little room for a few spare nuts and bolts and hose clips. A bottle of engine oil should be carried if a long journey is likely to lower the oil level

Useful items that can be squeezed into a small space: electrical cable and cable ties, ignition components, a windscreen wiper blade, hose clips, plus a fuel pump and coil are well worth having on board.

significantly, plus a bottle of coolant for top ups. Also, a bottle of cooling system sealant may be useful to combat sudden leakages until a proper repair can be made. Carry a torch, gloves and a few rags or wipes.

5. Your best policy

If you want to avoid problems, then you should of course make all the necessary checks prior to making your journey. Check all fluid levels, visible signs of leakage, condition of hoses and connections, tyres, electrical connections and operation of controls. Are there any strange noises or any other new maladies? Don't set off if you are at all in doubt about the health of your car.

At home

1. Tools

Here, you may have room for a complete set of tools to maintain your car and

A valve spring compressor is essential if you want to refurbish a cylinder head. Fortunately, not many specialised tools are required for most maintenance tasks.

more. However, you do not really need a great deal. A basic socket set, plus some open-ended and ring spanners, A/F sizes, screwdrivers, flat and Phillips headed, and some pliers comprise the main items. At home, you could also usefully keep a set of feeler gauges, a torque wrench, oil filter removing strap, timing light, compression gauge and multimeter. The rear axle will require a square-headed oil plug removing tool. You may find a carburettor airflow balancing meter useful to re-set the carburettor linkage after refurbishment. A grease gun is essential,

plus a small trolley jack and a pair of axle stands. A brake adjusting tool is also essential for the rear brakes. Unless you are embarking on a full restoration, the above items will cope with most requirements for home maintenance and repair.

2. Spares

As discussed earlier, the availability of spare parts for these cars is very good. There are many specialists who can supply a comprehensive catalogue of most of the things that you are likely

111

Autojumbler's delight. Spridget parts at bargain prices – the best prices on a wet day for the hardy.

to need. However, it should be noted that the spares available today are not necessarily from the original manufacturer or to exactly the same specification as the original part. There have been some quality issues, although generally, the availability and cost of spares is very good indeed.

Always check that the part you are replacing is correct for your model. The chances are that many components have been replaced previously, but was this with the correct item? Do not assume that the item you are replacing is original to the car – check the part numbers and refer to the vehicle VIN and spares catalogue before placing your order. Parts can also be purchased at specialist autojumbles and spares days. Both new and used original items can be found, and make for an interesting day out rummaging around the stalls for those hard to find and bargain items.

3. Other essentials

A good workshop manual and parts book are a must. If possible, try and obtain the original factory parts book for your model. These do turn up at autojumbles and online auction sites. Most current parts suppliers can supply a hard copy catalogue and provide an online service.

Original factory manuals, parts books, owner's handbook, suppliers' catalogues, reference lists, sales brochures ... you can never have too much reading and reference material. Original and period items can still be found at autojumbles, online, or through owners' clubs. New material is also available – this book, for instance!

18 The community

As a Spridget owner, you could hardly wish for a better level of support from the industry, clubs and fellow enthusiasts. For a full and up-to-date listing of clubs, services and reading matter, then the classic car magazines and the internet are both very good starting points. I would certainly recommend joining a recognised club, where you can obtain impartial advice from experienced enthusiasts. The following are just some of the better known organisations and companies. Indeed, I don't have space here to list all of the leading specialists and I must apologise to those I have omitted:

Clubs
Midget and Sprite Club, Stuart Watson, 'Staddlestones', Thicknall Lane, Clent, Stourbridge, West Midlands, DY9 0HX
Tel: 01562 883076 www.midgetandspriteclub.com

MG Owners' Club, Swavesey, Cambridge, CB4 5QZ
Tel: 01954 231125 www.mgownersclub.co.uk

MG Car Club, Kimber House, PO Box 251, Abingdon, Oxon, OX14 1FF Tel: 01235 555552 www.mgcc.co.uk

Austin-Healey Club UK www.austin-healey-club.com

Worldwide
North American MGB Register, PO Box 69, Eaton Rapids, MI 48827 USA www.mgcars.org.uk/namgbr

Sprite Car Club of Australia, PO Box 696. Kingswood 2747, NSW, Australia www.spriteclub.com

Austin-Healey Sprite Drivers Club, PO Box 248, Box Hill, Victoria 3128, Australia www.ahsdc.org

Austin Healey Club UK www.austin-healey-club.com/Pages/world-clubs

Austin-Healey Club America www.healeyclub.org/clubs

Amicale Spridget, 24 rue Paul Ratouis, 45650 Saint Jean le Blanc, France http://spridget.fr

Manufacturer's production records and archive
British Motor Industry Heritage Trust, Heritage Motor Centre, Banbury Road, Gaydon, Warwickshire, CV35 OBJ Tel: 01926 641188 www.heritage-motor-centre.co.uk

UK main spares suppliers
British Motor Heritage Ltd, Range Road, Cotswold Business Park, Witney, OX29 OYB Tel: 01993 707200
www.bmh-ltd.com/midgetparts.htm

Moss-Europe, Hampton Farm Estate, Hanworth, Middlesex, TW9 6DB Tel: 020 8867 2020
www.moss-europe.co.uk
Email: sales@moss-europe.co.uk

AH Spares Limited, Units 7 & 8 Westfield Rd, Kineton Road Industrial Estate, Southam, Warwickshire CV47 OJH Tel: 01926 817181
www.ahspares.co.uk

Frogeye Spares Co, Unit 338, Rushock Trading Estate, Rushock, Droitwich, Worcestershire WR9 ONR Tel: 01885 400791
www.frogeyespares.co.uk

Below: To celebrate 50 years of the MG Midget in 2011, around 700 Sprites and Midgets gathered at Burghley House in Lincolnshire. Despite being a very wet event, it was probably one of the largest-ever gatherings of Spridgets.

Above: Today, every stately home needs a complement of classic British sports cars. A fine collection of Spridgets in front of Burghley House.

Frontline Developments, 9 Station Yard, Steventon, Abingdon-on-Thames, Oxon, OX13 6RX
Tel: 01235 832632
www.frontlinedevelopments.com/mg

Peter May Engineering, Unit 4, Woodfield Business Units, Kidderminster Road, Ombersley, Worcestershire, WR9 OJH.
Tel: 01905 676185
www.petermayengineering.co.uk

Mike Authers Classics, Bramble Grange, Hanney Road, Steventon, Abingdon OX13 6AP Tel: 01235 834664
www.mgmidgets.com

US main spares suppliers
Victoria British Ltd, Box 14991, Lenexa, KS 66285-4991, USA Tel: (800)255-0088
www.longmotor.com

Moss Motors Ltd, PO Box 847, 440 Rutherford Street, Goleta, CA93116, USA Tel: (800) 667-7872 www.mossmotors.com

Australian main spares suppliers
The Bugeye Barn, 1/19 Fitzgerald St. Ferntree Gully, Victoria, Australia Tel: +61 (0)3 9758 8669 www.bugeyebarn.com

Colin Dodds Sprite Parts, 2 Parklea Close, Dural, NSW 2158 Australia Tel: +61 (0)4 1478 9263 www.spriteparts.com.au

A technical seminar day organised by the Midget and Sprite Club, at a Rover dealership, Mann Egerton in Surrey. A useful day that answered a lot of questions ... well, most anyway!

Magazines & books
MASCOT, the monthly magazine of the Midget and Sprite Club

Original Sprite and Midget ISBN: 978-1-906133337 (Terry Horler, Herridge & Sons)

Essential Buyers Guide, Midget & Sprite ISBN: 978-1-845843-54-0 (Terry Horler, Veloce Publishing Ltd)

MG Midget and Austin-Healey Sprite Restoration, Preparation & Maintenance (Osprey Automotive) ISBN: 978-1855322424 (Jim Tyler, Motorbooks International)

The MG Midget and Austin-Healey Sprite High-performance Manual ISBN: 978-1845841423 (Daniel Stapleton, Veloce Publishing Ltd)

Austin-Healey Sprite Gold Portfolio, 1958-1971 ISBN: 978-1855203716 (R M Clarke, Brooklands Books Ltd)

MG Midget Gold Portfolio, 1961-79 ISBN: 978-1855202283 (R M Clarke, Brooklands Books Ltd)

Spritely Years ISBN: 978-1852604981 (Tom Coulthard, Patrick Stephens Ltd)

More Healeys: Frog Eyes, Sprites and Midgets ISBN: 978-0856140495 (Geoffrey Healey, Haynes Publishing)

Mighty Midgets & Special Sprites ISBN: 978-1861261069 (John Baggot, The Crowood Press Ltd)

How to Power Tune Midget & Sprite for Road & Track ISBN: 978-1901295733 (Daniel Stapleton, Veloce Publishing Ltd)

Austin-Healey 'Frogeye' Sprite 1958-1961 Collection No.1 ISBN: 978-0946489206 (R M Clarke, Brooklands Books)

MG Midget 1961-1980 ISBN: 978-0946489862 (R M Clarke, Brooklands Books Ltd)

Austin-Healey Sprite 1958-1971 ISBN: 978-0907073406 (R M Clarke, Brooklands Books Ltd)

Austin-Healey 'Frogeye' Sprite Super Profile ISBN: 978-0854293438 (Lindsay Porter, G T Foulis & Co Ltd)

MG Midget, Austin-Healey Sprite Super Profile ISBN: 978-1845843540 (Lindsay Porter, Veloce Publishing Ltd)

Guide to Purchase & DIY Restoration of the MG Midget & Austin-Healey Sprite ISBN: 978-0854293360 (Lindsay Porter, G T Foulis & Co Ltd)

MG Midget Reborn ISBN: 978-0951073407 (Peter Berkin, Haidee Publications)

The Sprites and Midgets ISBN: 978-0900549533 (Eric Dymock, Motorbooks International

Practical Classics on Sprite/Midget Restoration ISBN: 978-0948207488 (R M Clarke, Brooklands Books)

Sprites & Midgets, The Complete Story ISBN: 978-1852235093 (Anders Ditlev Clausager, The Crowood Press)

MG & Austin-Healey Spridgets ISBN: 978-0902280960 (Chris Harvey, The Oxford Illustrated Press)

Note: A number of the books listed here are currently out of print, but are well worth looking out for on the secondhand market. Some have become collectors items in their own right – be prepared to pay the going price!

As a Spridget owner, get used to people approaching you with the words, "I used to own one of these." With 354,164 examples built and many changing hands ten times or more, this should not be unexpected. Many will then add, "I wish I still had mine."

And saving the worst for last, the author's own 'multi shades of red' Frogeye at the Heritage Motor Centre, Gaydon, to celebrate 50 years of the Austin-Healey Sprite in May 2008. Around 900 Sprites and Midgets attended. Almost certainly, the largest gathering of Spridgets ever.

Over the 21 years of production there were 14 distinct versions. The commonly applied Mk number does not necessarily identify a version clearly enough. Instead, the Car Number (VIN) prefix is an easier form of defining each Sprite or Midget by type. The following table lists these, along with the applicable engine for each version:

Version	Car no (VIN) prefix	Engine no prefix	Capacity/bhp	Number built
Sprite MkI May '58 to May '61	AN5 (Frogeye)	9C-U-H	948cc/42.5bhp	48987
Sprite MkII May '61 to Oct '62	HAN6	9CG-DA-H	948cc/46bhp	20450
Sprite MkII Oct '62 to Mar '64	HAN7 (disc front brakes)	10CG-DA-H	1098cc/55bhp	11215
Sprite MkIII Mar '64 to Sept '66	HAN8	10CC-DA-H	1098cc/59bhp	25905
Sprite MkIV Sept '66 to Oct '69	HAN9	12CC-DA-H 12CE-DA-H	1275cc/65bhp 1275cc/65bhp	20357
Sprite MkIV Oct '69 to Dec '70	HAN10 (Face-lift)	12CE-DA-H	1275cc/65bhp	1411
Austin Sprite Jan '71 to July '71	AAN10	12CE-DA-H	1275cc/65bhp	1022
Midget MkI June '61 to Oct '62	GAN1	9CG-DA-H	948cc/46bhp	16080
Midget MkI Oct '62 to Mar '64	GAN2 (disc front brakes)	10CG-DA-H	1098cc/55bhp	9601
Midget MkII Mar '64 to Sept '66	GAN3	10CC-DA-H	1098cc/59bhp	26601
Midget MkIII Sept '66 to Oct '69	GAN4	12CC-DA-H 12CE-DA-H	1275cc/65bhp	22415
Midget MkIII Oct '69 to Jan '72	GAN5 (Face-lift)	12CE-DA-H	1275cc/65bhp	29544
Midget MkIII Jan '72 to Oct '74	GAN5/105501 on (round rear wheelarch)	12V586FH 12V588FH 12V778FH	1275cc/65bhp	48287
Midget 1500 Oct '74 to Dec '79	GAN6 (rubber bumper)	FP	1493cc/65bhp	72289

The letter 'L' following the prefix denotes a left-hand drive version. From January 1969 and for North America, the 'L' was replaced with a 'U' and then followed by a year code letter. Hence, the VIN prefix for North American market Midgets became GAN5-U-A for

117

The car number (VIN) plate can be found just to the rear of the left-hand side front shock absorber. You may be asked for this number when ordering replacement parts.

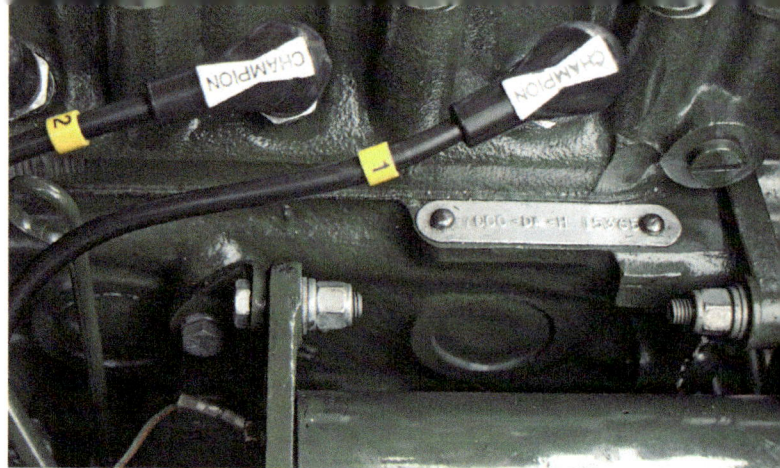

The A-series engine number plate is often missing following an engine rebuild. The prefix to the number identifies the exact specification of the engine. Without this, you will have a bit of detective work to do to identify the car.

1969 through to GAN6-U-M for 1979. Sprites and Midgets were assembled in Australia from a kit of parts sent from Abingdon, known as CKD kits, (completely knocked down). Australian assembled versions contained a 'Y' prefix to the VIN.

The last letter for the A-series engine number prefix denoted the compression ratio as either 'H' for high compression or 'L' for low compression. The engine number prefix for North American emissions control equipped A-series engines as compared to home market versions is as follows:

Home market	North America
12CC	12CD
12CE	12CJ
12V586FH	12V587ZL

12V588FH	12V671ZL
12V778FH	12V671ZL

The 1493cc Triumph engine for the Midget 1500 compared as follows:

FP (engine number)	E = Home market
FP (engine number)	UE = North America
FP (engine number)	UCE = California

The riveted engine number plate for the A-series engine is often removed when the engine is fully reconditioned. A new plate and number will be applied in the case of a factory reconditioned

Without the engine number plate, the original capacity of the A-series engine can at least be ascertained from this plate (or it may be cast into the cylinder) on the front left-hand side of the cylinder block.

The body number plate is fixed to the right-hand door pillar for the Sprite MkI and to the left-hand pillar for the later versions. Exactly why both a car and body number were applied to a vehicle of monocoque construction is one of life's little mysteries.

engine but otherwise, the engine may no longer have an identification number. The original capacity of the engine is shown on a plate, or else cast into the block, near the mechanical fuel pump boss on the front left-hand side. However, due to the many variations and applications of the A-series engine in BMC and BL vehicles, and the ease in swapping engines, it is not uncommon to find that a change to a non-original specification may have been made. This can cause some confusion and frustration, should an owner be unable to positively identify the exact engine type prior to carrying out work or purchasing parts. Factory reconditioned engines, termed 'Gold Seal' exchange units, were given new identification numbers with an 8G prefix.

The 1493cc engine was also used by Triumph in the Spitfire

and Dolomite, an FM or YG prefix will identify these respectively. The engine number is stamped into the cylinder block, at deck height, at the rear left-hand side.

The Sprite and Midget were the first MG sports cars to feature a monocoque, or unitary constructed, bodyshell. There was no separate chassis or sub frames; all major components were attached directly to the bodyshell. Oddly, MG retained the traditional practice of applying both a Car Number (VIN) and a body number. The body number appeared on a plate between the door hinges on the door pillar. This was on the right-hand side for the Sprite MkI and on the left-hand door pillar for all subsequent versions. The body number for the Midget 1500 can be found on the bonnet slam panel on later versions.

119

Factory reconditioned engines

The manufacturers provided their own reconditioned A-series engines in exchange for an original engine under their Gold Seal title. The engine number prefix system was changed to identify a Gold Seal replacement as follows:

Original prefix	Gold Seal prefix	Capacity	Application
9C-U-H	8G10	948cc	AN5
9CG-DA-H	8G16	948cc	HAN6/GAN1
9CG-DA-L	8G17	948cc	HAN6/GAN1
10CG-DA-H	8G124	1098cc	HAN7/GAN2
10CG-DA-L	8G125	1098cc	HAN7/GAN2
10CG-DA-H	8G135*	1098cc	HAN7/GAN2
10CG-DA-L	8G136*	1098cc	HAN7/GAN2
10CC-DA-H	8G150	1098cc	HAN8/GAN3
10CC-DA-L	8G149	1098cc	HAN8/GAN3
12CC-DA-H	8G180	1275cc	HAN9/GAN4
12CC-DA-L	8G179	1275cc	HAN9/GAN4
12CE-DA-H	8G180	1275cc	HAN9&10/GAN4&5
12CE-DA-L	8G179	1275cc	HAN9&10/GAN4&5
12V586FH	8G180	1275cc	GAN5
12V588FH	8G180	1275cc	GAN5
12V778FH	8G180	1275cc	GAN5
12CD-DA-H	8G189	1275cc	HAN9/GAN4
12CJ-DA-H	8G189	1275cc	HAN9/GAN4&5
12V587ZL	38G506	1275cc	GAN5
12V671ZL	38G506	1275cc	GAN5

The prefixes are followed by the individual engine number and then by a two letter suffix. The first suffix letter refers to the bore oversize, the second letter to the crankshaft re-grind undersize. The factory also offered a second tier level of reconditioned engine under their 'Silver Seal' label. These may be identified by the prefix: RKM.

8G135 and 8G136 engines are replacements for versions from August 1963. These featured larger inlet valves, revised combustion chambers and spigot locations for the inlet manifold.

20 Useful statistics

Tyre pressures

5.20 x 13 Crossply tyres

Front   18 psi (1.27kg/cm^2): normal running
         24 psi (1.69kg/cm^2): high speed running
Rear   20 psi (1.41kg/cm^2): normal running
         26 psi (1.83kg/cm^2): high speed running

145 x 13 Radial ply tyres

Front   22 psi (1.55kg/cm^2): normal running
         26 psi (1.83kg/cm^2): high speed running
Rear   24 psi (1.69kg/cm^2): normal running
         28 psi (1.97kg/cm^2): high speed running

Lubricants

Engine	20W/50
Gearbox	20W/50 (948cc, 1098cc & 1275cc)
Gearbox	EP 90 (1493cc)
Rear axle	EP 90
Steering rack & pinion	EP 90

Capacities

Engine oil	7 pints (4L) 948cc, 1098cc, 1275cc
	8 pints (4.6L) 1493cc
Gearbox oil	2.3 pints (1.3L) 948cc, 1098cc, 1275cc
	1.75 pints (1.0L) 1493cc
Rear axle oil	1.75 pints (1.0L)
Fuel tank	6 gallons (27.3L)
	7 gallons (31.8L) from GAN5/105501

Cooling system   10.5 pints (6.0L) including heater 948cc, 1098cc and early 1275cc engines with vertical flow radiators.
6 pints (3.4L) 1275cc engine with crossflow radiator.
7.5 pints (4.3L) including heater 1493cc engine.

Ignition

Firing order	1 - 3 - 4 - 2
Sparkplug gap	0.025in. (0.63mm)
Contact breaker gap	0.015in. (0.38mm)

Ignition timing

		(static degrees BTDC)	
		Compression: High	Low
Sprite MkI	948cc	5	1
Sprite MkII/Midget MkI	948cc	4	1
	1098cc	5	3 to 5
Sprite MkIII/Midget MkII	1098cc	5	3 to 5
Sprite MkIV/Midget MkIII	1275cc	7	4 to 7
Midget 1500	1493cc	10	0

Valve clearances

948cc, 1098cc & 1275cc
0.012in. (0.3mm) inlet and exhaust (cold)
1493cc
0.010in. (0.25mm) inlet and exhaust (cold)

Dimensions

	Sprite MkI	Sprite MkII to IV Midget MkI to III	Midget 1500
Length	11ft 0.6in (337cm)	11ft 5in (349cm)	11ft 9in
Width	4ft 5in (135cm)	**	4ft 7in
Height	4ft 2in (125cm)	4ft 6in (cm)	4ft 7in
Ground clearance	5in (12.7cm)	5in (12.7cm)	6in (15.3cm)
Turning circle	32ft (9.75m)	32ft (9.75m)	32ft (9.75m)

** The width of the Sprite MkIII and Midget MkII increased with the introduction of exterior door handles in March 1964; from 4ft 5in (135cm) to 4ft 7in (140cm).

Weights (Approx kerb weights)

Sprite MkI	948cc	1491lb/678kg
Sprite MkII/Midget MkI	948cc	1526lb/694kg
	1098cc	1526lb/697kg
Sprite MkIII/Midget MkII	1098cc	1581lb/719kg
Sprite MkIV/Midget MkIII	1275cc	1600lb/727kg
Midget 1500	1493cc	1720lb/782kg

Caring for your scooter

How to maintain & service your 49cc to 125cc twist & go scooter

Trevor Fry

ISBN: 978-1-845840-95-2

First aid for your car

Your expert guide to common problems & how to fix them

ISBN: 978-1-845845-19-3

Simple fixes for your car

How to do small jobs yourself and save money

Carl Collins

ISBN: 978-1-845845-18-6

For more info on Veloce titles, visit our website at www.veloce.co.uk
• email: info@veloce.co.uk • Tel: +44(0)1305 260068

Index